YORK NOTES

General Editors: ~~
of Stirling) & ~~
University of ~~

Arthur Conan Doyle

THE HOUND OF THE BASKERVILLES

Notes by Terence Brown
MA PH D (DUBLIN) FTCD
Director of Modern English, Trinity College, Dublin

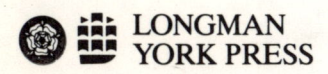

LONGMAN YORK PRESS

YORK PRESS
Immeuble Esseily, Place Riad Solh, Beirut.

LONGMAN GROUP LIMITED
London
Associated companies, branches and representatives throughout the world

© Librairie du Liban 1980

All rights reserved. No part of this publication may be reproduced, stored in a retrieval system, or transmitted in any form or by any means, electronic, mechanical, photocopying, recording, or otherwise, without the prior permission of the copyright owner.

First published 1980
ISBN 0 582 78128 0

Printed in Hong Kong by
Wing Tai Cheung Printing Co Ltd

Contents

Part 1: Introduction   *page* 5
   The life of Arthur Conan Doyle   5
   Sherlock Holmes in his historical context   8
   Conclusion   11
   A note on the text   12

Part 2: Summaries   13
   A general summary   13
   Detailed summaries   14

Part 3: Commentary   42
   Introduction   42
   The specific literary form of *The Hound of the Baskervilles*   42
   Suggested themes   44
   Literary techniques and strategies   49
   The characters   50
   The visual quality of *The Hound of the Baskervilles*   55
   Weaknesses of style, technique and plot   57

Part 4: Hints for study   59
   Study projects   64

Part 5: Suggestions for further reading   65

The author of these notes   66

Part 1

Introduction

The life of Arthur Conan Doyle

Arthur Conan Doyle was born of Irish parents in Edinburgh in 1859. The fact of his Irish parentage often comes as a surprise to readers who have always thought of the creator of Sherlock Holmes and Dr Watson as a typical late-Victorian English gentleman. His love of cricket and zest for all field games, his support of the British war-effort against the Boers in South Africa, his bluff, hearty appearance, his straightforward concern for fair-play in life as well as in sport all suggest something approaching a caricature of English manhood. In fact, as is often the case, the Scot or the Irishman contrives to achieve a condition of typical Englishness that the native-born Englishman rarely attempts. One senses something of this kind when reflecting on the career of Conan Doyle, considering how the Scots-trained doctor of Irish Catholic background achieved success and public esteem in Victorian and Edwardian England. Both Conan Doyle's parents were of direct Irish extraction. Indeed, his uncle Henry became manager of the National Gallery in Dublin. His grandfather had left Dublin for London in 1815; his father, a civil servant and spare-time painter, had accepted a civil service job in Edinburgh where he married Mary Foley, who bore him a large family. Arthur was the first child of the marriage.

Despite his father's impracticalities in financial matters and despite the family's comparative poverty, Conan Doyle was given a sound, if occasionally over-strict, education. He was instructed by the Catholic priests of the Jesuit Order at Stonyhurst College in England where, although he was later to leave the faith in which he was educated, the strong-minded, perhaps harsh, discipline grounded him in habits of hard work without regard for immediate comfort which were to serve him well in his later life as a prolific writer and much sought-after public speaker. It was at school that Conan Doyle first encountered the historical writings of Thomas Babington Macaulay (1800–59) and the novels of Sir Walter Scott (1771–1832). These awakened his interest in history, to which subject he devoted so much of his imaginative life as a writer.

Conan Doyle entered the University of Edinburgh in 1876, qualifying as Bachelor of Medicine in 1881 despite the financial hardship which necessitated temporary jobs to enable him to pay his university fees. One of his professors at Edinburgh, Dr Bell, impressed him much as a man of unusual deductive powers and it was Bell who was later to serve as a model for Sherlock Holmes himself. At Edinburgh Conan Doyle also met a strange, volatile, eccentric, violently emotional individual named George Budd, a fellow medical student. Perhaps Sherlock Holmes's eccentricities of behaviour, his obvious disregard for conventional manners and regulations which sometimes so surprised the loyal Dr Watson, were suggested to Conan Doyle by his friend's peculiarities. Conan Doyle was attracted to Budd and after a brief adventure as a ship's surgeon on a ship bound for the West Coast of Africa, agreed to embark upon the altogether more risky venture of going into partnership with Budd in a medical practice in Plymouth in the south of England. The oddity of Budd's medical advice can be judged from this example of his consulting-room behaviour. He was confronted by an overweight patient. Budd grabbed him by his waistcoat and forced him into the street with the words 'You eat too much, drink too much, and sleep too much! Knock down a policeman and come again when they let you out.' On another occasion he was consulted by a woman who complained of a 'sinking feeling'. She was instructed to take her medicine 'and if that does no good, swallow the cork, for there is nothing better when you are sinking.' There is something of Holmes's cavalier unwillingness to suffer fools gladly in this behaviour. Conan Doyle approved of Budd rather as Dr Watson does of Holmes in the author's fiction, but probably with more misgivings since his own financial well-being depended on the partnership.

Before long Conan Doyle's misgivings had the better of the admiration he felt for his remarkable partner. As the practice declined the friends quarreled. Conan Doyle left Plymouth for another southern coastal town, Portsmouth, where he set up in practice on his own account in July 1882. It was here he married, played his part in the local community, especially on the sports fields, and began his career as a writer. His practice, while fairly successful, never brought him much more than a sufficient income, and, as his children were born and added to his financial responsibilities, it was with an eye to augmenting his income as well as with hopes of literary success that he began sending out his stories to magazines in hopes of publication and payment. He wrote one novel which was lost in the post on its way to a publisher, then immediately wrote another, which, while escaping the dismal fate of his first effort, was no luckier in the matter of finding a willing publisher. It was with these disappointments in mind and with only a few pieces in the *Cornhill* and *Blackwood's* magazines to encourage his hopes, that Conan Doyle wrote a novel, *A Study in Scarlet* (1886), where Sherlock Holmes made his first appearance. Like many a young author, Conan Doyle did not realise what an asset his new character was to prove and sold the copyright on the book for a mere £25, no doubt thinking that the historical novel *Micah Clarke*, which he began while waiting for *A Study in Scarlet* to be published, was altogether a more important enterprise.

Conan Doyle always aspired to be a serious novelist, a writer of historical fictions which might be worthy successors to Sir Walter Scott's masterpieces. It was a constant source of irritation to him that the reading public much preferred his detective stories to his more considered works like *Micah Clarke* or his novel *The White Company*, set in the reign of Edward III, for both of which he had done much careful historical research.

In 1891, after a brief visit to Vienna, Conan Doyle settled in London where he hoped to establish himself as an oculist. Finding that this occupation did not really provide a sufficient income, he was forced to depend increasingly on his pen to maintain himself and his family.

The idea of writing short stories with a recurrent central character seemed a financially worthwhile venture to Conan Doyle since he knew that an increasing volume of passengers on Britain's railway system had created a large new readership for immediately entertaining magazine fiction. Magazines such as *The Strand* had begun to cater for this new literary market and Conan Doyle astutely realised that he could contribute to it, cleverly realising that serialised fiction concerning one central character, with each episode complete in itself, could have particular attractions for editors and for readers:

> Considering these various journals with their disconnected stories, it had struck me that a single character running through a series, if it only engaged the attention of the reader, would bind that reader to that particular magazine. On the other hand, it had long seemed to me that the ordinary serial might be an impediment rather than a help to a magazine since, sooner or later, one missed one number and afterwards it had lost all interest. Clearly the ideal compromise was a character which carried through, and yet instalments which were each complete in themselves, so that the purchaser was always sure that he could relish the whole contents of the magazine. I believe that I was the first to realise this and *The Strand Magazine* the first to put it into practice.

The stories were popular beyond Conan Doyle's wildest hopes. For a variety of reasons (see below) the personality of Sherlock Holmes appealed enormously to late-Victorian readers. Soon Holmes and Watson were household names, characters beloved of readers throughout the British Isles and in America. Today the names Conan Doyle and Sherlock Holmes are indissolubly linked in the public mind.

Between 1886 and 1891 Conan Doyle regularly published Sherlock Holmes stories until he became heartily sick of the character that had brought him financial security, so eventually he felt driven to dispatch Holmes by the expedient of sending him to his death over the Reichenbach Falls in Switzerland: 'I couldn't revive him if I would, at least not for years, for I have had such an overdose of him that I feel towards him as I do towards *pâté de foie gras*, of which I once ate too much, so that the name of it gives me a sickly feeling to this day'. For years after Conan Doyle was urged by the public (many readers wrote him imploring letters) and by his editor to produce yet another tale of the amazing Sherlock Holmes. Conan Doyle obliged in 1901 and published *The Hound of the Baskervilles* (a story suggested to him by an account of a Devonshire legend of a ghostly Dartmoor hound) in *The Strand Magazine* from August 1901 to April 1902. Conan Doyle attempted to persuade his public that the story recounted an early adventure of Sherlock Holmes who remained very definitely dead, but the public was unconvinced and no one was surprised when, in October 1903, *The Strand* began a new series with the detective fully restored to life. Conan Doyle published his last Sherlock Holmes story, the sixtieth, in *The Strand* in 1927.

Conan Doyle spent much of the rest of his literary life attempting to achieve finally what he had always so desired, a reputation as a serious author. The success of the Holmes stories had made this almost impossible, despite his strenuous efforts. In the midst of a vigorous life as a sportsman, lecturer, traveller and public man, prospective Member of Parliament and, in his last years, convinced evangelist for spiritualism, he sought to write the work by which he might be remembered as something more than the creator of Sherlock Holmes. But it is not for his historical romances we remember him, nor for his six-volume history of the Great War, nor for any of his other stories. Only the tales he thought of rather slightingly, the tales of a brilliant sleuth and his dogged comrade, assure him of the affection of countless readers.

Sherlock Holmes in his historical context

The remarkable success that Conan Doyle achieved with his detective hero may be related by the critic and historian to many of the conditions of late-Victorian English society, and to the hopes, aspirations and fears of the late-Victorian middle-class. Sherlock Holmes might be described as a late-Victorian cult-figure of the kind our own century has created in television series and in films such as the James Bond fantasies that were screened in many countries in the 1960s. Works of this kind often reflect contemporary attitudes and opinions much more obviously than do works by serious artists. The serious artist is usually an individual with a unique, socially disruptive, extraordinary view of the world, whereas the writer of best-selling, popular novels or the director of popular films and television series is most often notable for his capacity to identify and exploit the commonplace preoccupations and fantasies of his contemporaries without really disturbing conventional minds. Conan Doyle was a writer of the latter type, deeply representative in his life of English middle-class tastes, prejudices and desires, whose popular fictions managed to fulfil the imaginative needs of a middle-class readership anxious for entertainment and distraction. The following are ways in which Sherlock Holmes as hero fulfilled some of the needs of his admiring audience.

Holmes has a clear sense of right and wrong

To most people most periods have been disturbing, frightening, morally complicated and confusing, so it can often be a serious error for a literary historian to relate aspects of a literary work to the troubled times in which it was produced. The last two decades of the nineteenth century in England, however, may properly be described as particularly confusing for English middle-class men and women. The widespread availability of information in newspapers and magazines allowed the ordinary citizen a sense, that he may not have had in earlier periods, of the complexity and ambiguity of the world in which he lived. New ideas about the nature and origins of man, that had circulated in academic and intellectual circles for some thirty years, had begun to disturb the minds of even suburban householders; doubts about the supernatural basis of the moral law were no longer easily dismissed. The major English cities were places where the middle-classes sought refuge in safe suburbs from the great numbers of the poor, the unemployed, from criminal and violent people. Crime was commonplace, the Law often incapable of protecting a householder's person or property. In such a context Sherlock Holmes's precise, assured sense of right and wrong, his ability to know crime for what it is and to unmask and punish it (sometimes with little attention to due legal process) must have been very cheering indeed, fulfilling basic human needs for a sense of security in a morally and socially insecure world. Holmes in the stories is in control, capable, largely untroubled by ethical or legal dilemmas, a man of action.

Holmes is an amateur and a gentleman

Victorian society was obsessed by the idea of class. Railway trains, for example, were divided into First, Second and Third and Ladies Only carriages, so that the respectable might not have to encounter the disreputable, nor any lady be addressed in a compromising manner. The condition of being a gentleman was much considered and much sought after. Aristocratic birth was not the only means of achieving that social status, though it was the simplest. Less fortunate men, who could not lay claim to gentle birth, might achieve social success through creating the impression that they had no reason to work for a living. Individuals who maintained such a position of social eminence usually depended on capital generated by mercantile and entrepreneurial effort but it was very necessary to disguise this fact. Any work undertaken by such a personage had to seem as the eccentric manifestation of an enthusiastic nature. No hint could be given that work was necessary. Many of the middle-classes who had not the financial resources to sustain such a life undoubtedly envied the apparently indolent lives of those who could, whilst aspiring and perhaps insecurely pretending to that happy state. Sherlock Holmes, who, we learn from the early stories, does in fact have to work for a living and whose manner of life is not one likely to be sustained by modest expenditures, always manages to give the impression that he only takes on a case when it interests him and that he is not interested in the matter of his fee. He is the amateur, the gentleman who works when he chooses, the man of style and social assurance who has escaped the vulgar constraints of the market-place. At least, such is the impression he desires to create. In this he was not so far removed from the neuroses and anxieties of many of his readers.

Sherlock Holmes is an individualist

This aspect of the character, related to the fact that he is presented as an amateur, may well have appealed to his readers, many of whom depended on a professional police force for their sense of security in a violent world. The appeal of such a figure as Holmes is that he has the courage and ability to take the pursuit and punishment of the criminal into his own hands. He is a free-lance artist with a cavalier disregard for what he sees as the slow-witted procedures of the police-force. In some of the early tales, indeed, he is seen working against the police.

To an audience that must occasionally have suspected that there was a certain lack of manliness and courage implicit in its dependence on the police for safety, Sherlock Holmes was attractive because of his willingness to solve problems through immediate personal action.

Holmes is a man of assured cultivation

He has developed aesthetic tastes, is appreciative of the arts. He seems to move easily in the world of art galleries and music. In this way he must have seemed an idealised version of the kind of person many of his readers might have wished to be. Late-Victorian society offered increased educational and cultural opportunities for ordinary middle-class people, opening up the world of letters, music and art to larger numbers of people than in the past. An individual could compensate for a lack of really significant social or financial success through the acquisition of artistic cultivation without any great commitment to the rigours of the intellectual life. Holmes the accomplished violinist, the artistic connoisseur, the attender at musical concerts has just the necessary degree of cultivation to make him an attractive rather than intimidating figure to readers who wished to identify themselves with amateur accomplishment. In modern thrillers the hero often displays an intimate knowledge of wine and high cuisine, satisfying the reader's needs for wish-fulfilment. Holmes's knowledge of the arts, his cultivation, serve a similar function in Conan Doyle's stories.

Conclusion

(1) Arthur Conan Doyle was a writer who hoped for a reputation as a serious writer.
(2) He wrote the Sherlock Holmes stories with a specific audience in mind and his intentions were commercial rather than artistic (he was more serious about his historical romances).
(3) Sherlock Holmes appealed to late-Victorian readers because
   (*a*) He has a clear sense of right and wrong
   (*b*) He is an amateur and a gentleman
   (*c*) He is an individualist
   (*d*) He is a cultivated connoisseur of the arts.

Nothing described so far would have guaranteed the success of the Sherlock Holmes stories, if Conan Doyle had not been a capable, entertaining writer, well able to manage a plot, to raise and maintain suspense in a chapter and between episodes, so holding a reader's attention.

A note on the text

The best text, since it contains Paget's illustrations, is *The Annotated Sherlock Holmes*, edited with an Introduction, Notes and Bibliography by William S. Baring-Gould, John Murray, London, 1968. This is a two-volume work (*The Hound of the Baskervilles* is in Volume II) which contains much valuable information. However, the student should beware. Many books and articles about the Sherlock Holmes stories indulge in the playful, but often irritating, pretence that Holmes and Watson were real people, with real biographies. A great deal of ink has been spilt in trying to account for all the oddities of chronology and geography that reveal themselves in the stories once the reader begins to imagine that the main characters were actual people. Conan Doyle, of course, made no real effort to create consistent biographies for them. So many of the notes to the above volume are playful efforts to achieve consistency where there was no effort to be consistent. The best easily available text is the Pan Book edition, London and Sydney, 1957. This edition has an excellent foreword and afterword by the contemporary English novelist, John Fowles.

Part 2

Summaries
of THE HOUND OF THE BASKERVILLES

A general summary

The novel recounts the adventures of Holmes and Watson in pursuit of the murderer of Sir Charles Baskerville. The story is told by Dr Watson, Holmes's faithful if dim-witted companion. He tells how Holmes was approached by a Devonshire doctor named Mortimer who recounts the tale of the Baskerville curse, a murderous, supernatural hound. Mortimer reveals the mysterious events surrounding Sir Charles Baskerville's recent death. It seems the curse of the Baskervilles has struck again, for beside Sir Charles's body were found the footsteps of an enormous hound. Sir Henry, the last of the Baskervilles, has returned to London from South America, where he was born, to enter into his inheritance. Whilst in London two of his boots disappear in mysterious circumstances, one, a new boot, turns up again almost immediately, the other, an old one, does not. Holmes and Watson fail to capture or identify the spy who has been watching Sir Henry since he arrived in London, only glimpsing his black beard.

Sir Henry and Watson journey to Devonshire to Baskerville Hall while Holmes apparently remains in London. In Devon Watson observes the inhabitants of the Hall and the surrounding countryside, recording events in his journal, and sending regular reports to Holmes. Suspicion is at first directed to Mr and Mrs Barrymore, two servants in Baskerville Hall, who behave very strangely. It seems Mr Barrymore rises at night and is clearly about some strange business of his own. Sir Henry develops romantic feelings for a neighbour, the sister of a rather eccentric naturalist named Stapleton. There is also an escaped convict on the moor, a dangerous criminal who has escaped from the great Dartmoor prison.

The mystery of the Barrymores is solved fairly quickly by Dr Watson. They are in league with the escaped prisoner, a man named Selden, who is Mrs Barrymore's younger brother. They hope to help him to escape to South America. Watson catches a glimpse of another man on the moor, a mysterious stranger. This turns out to be Sherlock Holmes who has been living on the moor keeping watch on the villain, the naturalist Stapleton, who is, it turns out, married to the lady who poses as his sister. Out on the moor Holmes and Watson hear the great hound baying in pursuit of a man. Stapleton has won, it seems; Sir Henry is killed by the dog. But no, it is Selden who has suffered this horrible fate. Barrymore had supplied him with one of Sir Henry's old suits and this is the cause of his doom. Holmes knows, as we learn later, that Stapleton is a Baskerville with designs on the estate. He will certainly repeat his attempt on Sir Henry's life. So Holmes, after he unearths all the facts relating to Sir Charles's murder, uses Sir Henry as a bait for Stapleton, suggesting he dine with the evil man and afterwards walk home across the moor. This he does, where he is chased by the fiery hound that Stapleton has released. Holmes is in wait and shoots the hound, but not before it has leapt at Sir Henry's throat, frightening him terribly. The horrible appearance of the hound was caused by a coating of phosphorus. Stapleton, knowing he is discovered, flees across the Great Mire where it is presumed he drowns. Holmes finds Sir Henry's boot which Stapleton has used to put his hound on to Sir Henry's scent.

Detailed summaries

Chapter 1: Mr Sherlock Holmes

Holmes and Watson make the acquaintance of Dr Mortimer after speculating about his identity.

COMMENTARY: Chapter 1 must serve two purposes, (*i*) it must allow readers to meet Sherlock Holmes again, and (*ii*) it must begin to whet the reader's appetite for the events to come. So in this chapter we see Holmes and Watson playing out the roles familiar to readers of the earlier works; Holmes the searchingly perceptive sleuth, Watson the dogged faithful worshipper at the shrine of Holmes's great intellect. The opening sentence is suggestive of Watson's respectful loyalty and sense of privilege in being associated with so great a man as Holmes. 'Mr Sherlock Holmes, who was usually very late in the mornings, save upon those not infrequent occasions when he stayed up all night, was seated at the breakfast table.' The tone is one of respectful revelation. Watson, the narrator, naturally assumes that the public will wish to know details about their hero such as the hour at which he customarily breakfasts. The tone also suggests a certain smug satisfaction on Watson's part that he is the one who is so intimate with the great man that he attends upon him at breakfast-time. He calls Holmes 'Mr Sherlock Holmes', as if revealing him to a public which must be kept slightly at a distance, though the next time Watson speaks of his hero it is as the much more familiar 'Holmes'. The audience is also teased by two questions. What does Holmes do in the evenings that accounts for his usually sleeping late, and even more stimulating, what was he doing on those 'not infrequent occasions when he stayed up all night'? One of the major strengths of Conan Doyle as a writer is his quite remarkable economy, his ability to say much in short space and in this arresting opening sentence we have a prime example of this skill. The relationship of Holmes and Watson, the intermediary role Watson plays between the audience and the sleuth, and the mysterious brilliancy of Holmes's intellectual life are all suggested in the space of twenty-nine words.

This introductory sentence complete, we are immediately presented with Holmes and Watson in a familiar routine. A strange object has presented itself for Holmes's attention. Watson picks it up and describes it to us, while Holmes continues breakfasting. The reader senses that Holmes has already deduced its source, while Watson is ponderously reaching only elementary conclusions about the stick's owner. Watson's rather slow thought processes are suggested in the one word 'occupation'. The act of picking up and looking at a walking stick could hardly be described as such unless inspecting and contemplating it was being undertaken in a particularly ponderous way.

The routine develops in familiar ways. Holmes interrogates the slow-witted Watson about the stick. To Watson's rather painstaking rehearsals of the obvious he replies 'Good', 'Excellent', 'Perfectly sound', concluding with a fine compliment, as if he knows the answer and is delighted to discover his friend's ability to arrive at the same truth. Poor stolid Watson is so gratified by Holmes's warm praise that he doesn't notice how gratuitously insulting his hero has been. For it is not that he has already deduced the truth about the stick but that he has not yet taken the trouble, believing it to be the work of a moment that can wait satisfactory completion of the morning meal (notice that there is no more mention of the silver coffee pot). He examines the stick with the naked eye, only then does 'an expression of interest' cross his face and only then does he examine the thing with a magnifying glass. To that moment he has been playing with Watson and using him, as he is to do in a much more extensive way later in the book. Holmes then frankly states the truth: 'When I said that you stimulated me I meant to be frank, that in noting your fallacies I was occasionally guided towards the truth.'

By now the reader has become intrigued, not simply by the skilfully suggested relationship between Holmes and Watson but by the Penang lawyer walking stick itself. It has allowed us to see Holmes at work

16 · Summaries

employing his famous deductive skills and we sense that the action is about to begin, as it very appropriately does when the stick's owner, Dr James Mortimer, arrives on the doorstep of Holmes's Baker Street home. The arrival is, of course, a preposterously opportune piece of plotting by Conan Doyle, but for a reader this is part of the pleasure; a conventional form allows a character to turn up just when he is needed and a reader is gratified rather than irritated by such obvious authorial strategies. So Holmes is allowed a properly melodramatic speech—'Now is the dramatic moment of fate, Watson, when you hear a step upon the stair which is walking into your life, and you know not whether for good or ill.' So warned, we await the opening of the door.

We are then introduced to Dr James Mortimer. Most of *The Hound of the Baskervilles* is cast in the form of narrative and dialogue but as each new minor character appears the author provides us with a brief thumb-nail sketch. These are all very significant for they establish the characters' identities for us and throughout the book we tend to respond to each of them in terms of these initial impressions. On this occasion we are introduced to a character in terms which suggest decency and trustworthiness. Mortimer's eyes are 'keen', they sparkle, 'brightly from behind gold-rimmed glasses' and he has a 'general air of peering benevolence'. Furthermore he dresses correctly but without any suggestion of punctilious vanity; the quality of his clothes suggests a measure of material disinterest as Holmes has already prophesied. His enthusiastic pleasure in retrieving his property suggests an impulsive warm-hearted nature. All in all he is a man to trust.

Mortimer reveals himself to be a man of scientific cast of mind, a specialist in the forms of the human skull. He has apparently reached the limits of scientific knowledge and has been driven to seek the assistance of a man who is capable of going where it seems science cannot. The chapter ends as we await his tale.

NOTES AND GLOSSARY
Penang lawyer: a kind of stick weighted with lead; could be used as a weapon
ferrule: a ring of metal round the stick to prevent splitting
MRCS: Member of the Royal College of Surgeons
visiting-card: a card with one's name and address on it; usually left when visiting
mastiff: a giant smooth-coated dog, once used as a hunt dog
frock-coat: a double-breasted coat reaching to about the knees
consulting practice: a medical practice, to which doctors refer patients for specialised treatment

Summaries · 17

Chapter 2: The Curse of the Baskervilles

Dr Mortimer tells Holmes and Watson about the eighteenth-century manuscript and reads its contents to them. They learn of the tragic events that surrounded the death of Hugo Baskerville and of the curse of the Baskerville line. Dr Mortimer then reads from a more recent document, a newspaper report of the death of Sir Charles Baskerville. Dr Mortimer has other mysterious facts to add to the public account of Sir Charles's death, for he had personally examined the place of death, finding there the footprints of an enormous hound. This fact was concealed at the coroner's inquest.

COMMENTARY: Chapter 2 begins quietly, with an air of scholarly enquiry, of rationality and balanced assessment of evidence. Dates and styles of penmanship absorb Holmes's mind, while Mortimer informs us that he is 'shrewd, practical and unimaginative'. This atmosphere of judicious assessment and concern for detail and fact serves as a clever introduction to the chilling tale Mortimer is about to rehearse. The bizarre, hair-raising tale that follows is set in a context of scientific enquiry which renders it much more disturbing than if Chapter 2 had immediately plunged us into an account of the strange events surrounding Sir Charles Baskerville's untimely and tragic death.

Chapter 2 has begun by lowering the tension generated at the end of Chapter 1. A reader senses that the author is almost teasing him, forcing him to read on to satisfy his curiosity, which mounts as the moment of revelation is postponed. At last Mortimer asserts that his business is pressing, that it demands a decision within twenty-four hours but that he must first read the document he has brought with him, for it is 'intimately connected with the affair'. Now Mortimer could, of course, have summarised its contents for Holmes and Watson, thus allowing his pressing business to be dealt with all the more quickly, but that would have been much less exciting and suggestive. So we are allowed to hear the 'curious old world document' with Mortimer's 'high crackling voice' in our ears and with three questions in our minds—What is the decision that must be taken in the immediate future? What does the document contain and how do its contents relate to Mortimer's immediate problems?

Having decided to use the literary expedient of an historical document (oddly we are not told how Mortimer came to possess it but in our impatience to hear its contents we don't notice that) Conan Doyle exploits its possibilities to the full, providing us with a tale of gothic horror. Perhaps the whole thing is a little overdone, but there is no denying that we read this compulsive tale of violence, revenge and occult horror with little opportunity to remark its rather crude melodramatic effects and its inept attempt to suggest an eighteenth-century manner ('Whereat Hugo ran from the house ...'). The situation is compelling: Holmes the famous sleuth, Watson the honest doctor, Mortimer the practical man of science reading aloud from the 'yellow paper' with 'its faded script'. We are held in thrall, so that it is a real shock as the tale ends to realise suddenly that Holmes is merely bored. So superior a being he seems at such a moment, coolly tossing a cigarette-end into the fire with a yawn, unmoved by Mortimer's ghastly tale. It is fact and the present that hold his attention, not superstitions from the past. To the account of Sir Charles's death in a recent local newspaper, the *Devon County Chronicle*, he gives his rapt attention but to a tale of a supernatural curse he responds with condescending disinterest.

The eighteenth-century document allows Conan Doyle to introduce the supernatural atmosphere which is to predominate in much of the book. It does not supply us with much information. The newspaper account, on the other hand, much more protracted and detailed than such a newspaper piece is customarily likely to be, serves as a straightforward technique for establishing much of the basic information a reader will need as the plot of the book unfolds. The article tells us of Sir Charles's short occupancy of Baskerville Hall, of his fortune, of his childlessness, and of the doubts and rumours that surrounded his death. We learn of his domestic arrangements, of his bad heart and attacks of nervous depression, and we learn that Dr Mortimer was both his friend and medical attendant. We learn of the hour, the place and manner of Sir Charles's death, of the discovery of the body, with its strangely contorted features, of the post-mortem and the coroner's verdict. We hear for the first time of the heir to the estate and fortune, Sir Charles's as yet undiscovered younger brother. At last Holmes is interested; he asks for further information, assuming that Mortimer knows more or he should not have come to consult him.

Mortimer's account of the private facts associated with Sir Charles's death begins quietly enough. We hear of other men of education in the late Sir Charles's neighbourhood, of his scientific interests and retiring nature, but also, as the tension mounts again, of his nervous, morbid fears of the family curse. Suddenly the excitement reaches a crescendo as we hear of the night of the mysterious death, how Mortimer was called out to view the corpse and how he could verify all Barrymore's testimony before the coroner save for one appalling detail, the footprints. When Holmes asks 'A man or a woman?' we already know the fateful answer. With a delicious blend of expectation and plain fright we read: 'Mr Holmes, they were the footprints of a gigantic hound!'

NOTES AND GLOSSARY

The Great Rebellion: the English Civil War between Charles I and Parliament, 1642–6; it was followed by the second Civil War of 1648–51

Lord Clarendon: Edward Hyde, Earl of Clarendon, 1608–1674; English Royalist statesman; wrote *The True Historical Narrative of the Rebellion and Civil Wars in England*, 1702–4

yeoman: a respectable man of high but not noble birth, who owned and worked farming land

leagues: a measurement of distance; in England about three miles

wench: a peasant girl

flagons: containers holding a supply of drink for use at table; they often have a handle, spout and lid

trencher: a broad or wooden platter on which to serve food

Devon County Chronicle: the name of a local newspaper

nouveaux riches: (*French*) the new rich, a class customarily despised

scion: a descendant

dyspnoea: medical term meaning difficulty of breathing

post-mortem: medical examination to determine cause of death when death is due to other than natural causes

coroner's jury: a court with a jury meets to consider and decide on the evidence, in the event of unnatural death, under the guidance of an official known as the coroner

gig: a light one-horse carriage

Chapter 3: The Problem

Holmes interrogates Dr Mortimer about the affair. Mortimer tells him that before Sir Charles's death a hound corresponding to the demon of the Baskerville legend had been seen on the moor. Dr Mortimer then informs Holmes and Watson that Sir Henry, Sir Charles's heir, is expected immediately. Henry is the last of the Baskervilles who has returned from abroad to enter into his inheritance. Dr Mortimer is worried about Sir Henry's safety in Devonshire. Holmes agrees to meet Sir Henry on the following morning, by which time he will have made up his mind on how to proceed with the matter. Watson leaves Holmes to meditate alone all day, returning in the evening to learn that Holmes has been studying a large-scale map of Devonshire. He has concluded

20 · Summaries

that Sir Charles was waiting for somebody on the moor on the night of his death.

COMMENTARY: The contemporary English novelist John Fowles has wittily suggested of *The Hound of the Baskervilles* that the 'least read chapter-title in all literature is the one that heads Chapter 3'. He means, of course, that a reader, in his anxiety to race ahead to discover what happens next, has little inclination to bother with such apparently unimportant matters as chapter headings. And now, as if to satisfy a reader's highly stimulated curiosity, Conan Doyle provides an extended passage of hectic interrogation and reply. Fact after fact spills out in a swift-moving dialogue in great contrast to the measured exposition of the plot in Chapters 1 and 2. Mortimer is excited, Watson is excited, the reader is excited and Holmes is now excited ('his eyes had the hard, dry glitter which shot from them when he was keenly interested') and all combine in a rapt attentiveness to the facts of the case. The reader should pay great attention to these, for here Conan Doyle is laying before us, as Mortimer lays before Holmes, the problem that must be solved. And since a good deal of the fun in reading this kind of fiction is to see if we can spot the villain before the hero does, we must attend to every clue. Conan Doyle however cleverly directs our attention away from the scientific weighing of facts, away from rational explanations. He does this by keeping the possibility well to the fore that Sir Charles may have died at the hands of supernatural agencies. Even the coolly analytic Dr Mortimer, who Holmes-like has estimated how long Sir Charles stood by the wicket-gate on the night of his death, cannot put the supernatural possibility from his mind. He expands upon his fears and confusion, thereby drawing attention away from the facts into the realms of rumour, superstition and gothic possibility.

Then, just as a reader begins to weigh supernatural and natural explanations of the strange events, the focus of the narrative is briskly altered. Attention is shifted to the question of Sir Charles's heir and to the dangers surrounding his imminent arrival.

Holmes certainly believes that a supernatural cause of death must be discounted and he is beginning to think that the case will involve him in the unmasking of criminality. Watson leaves him alone to ponder the affair. The plot here allows Conan Doyle to offer his readers a quickly-drawn sketch of eccentric genius at work. Watson leaves in mid-morning and returns towards nine o'clock in the evening. The room is full of smoke from 'the acrid fumes of strong, coarse tobacco'. Holmes is still in his famous dressing-gown, which presumably he was wearing to breakfast. He has obviously become so absorbed that he has neglected his clothing, food and the condition of the atmosphere. But lest this indifference to comfort and environment seem mere freakish eccentricity Conan Doyle also suggests strengths (he smokes 'strong, coarse tobacco' which almost suffocates poor Watson, who apparently lacks Holmes's physical capacities as well as his mental ones). There are reserves of energy and power present (Holmes is 'coiled up in an armchair').

This chapter, in contrast to the first two, ends quietly. You will remember that both Chapters 1 and 2 began rather quietly and then moved to points of high tension and excitement. Here the chapter begins with compulsive excitement and concludes with the tension somewhat relaxed. This was a clever ploy on the author's part, for a reader would quickly become a little irritated if each chapter was seen to be a deliberate working up of his feelings to a point of cliff-hanging suspense. The ending of Chapter 3, with Holmes defining the problem thus far, before he turns to the intellectual satisfactions of his violin, allows a reader the luxury of savouring the full measure of the mystery he has been allowed to consider, as it encourages an expansive sense of the pleasurable excitements to come: 'The thing takes shape, Watson. It becomes coherent.'

NOTES AND GLOSSARY
sheep-dog: a dog trained to herd sheep
wicket-gate: a small gate, usually near a larger one
clogs: wooden shoes
farrier: a man who shoes horses
demon: Conan Doyle uses the word here in the Christian sense to mean an evil spirit, a servant of Satan
Father of Evil: Satan or the Devil
Waterloo Station: one of the major London railway stations
trustee and executor: individuals who have been appointed to execute and protect the terms of a will
black sheep of the family: the one that goes astray
club: a gentleman's club in London which offers dining and residential facilities with social exclusiveness
ordnance map: a one-inch scale map prepared for military purposes by the Ordnance Survey.

Chapter 4: Sir Henry Baskerville

We meet Sir Henry Baskerville and learn something of his character. We hear of the strangely composed message he has received and he is told of the events which surrounded Sir Charles's death and of the curse which hangs over his family. We also learn of Sir Henry's missing boot and the chapter concludes with Holmes and Watson discovering but failing to apprehend or recognise the black-bearded individual who has been following Sir Henry in London.

COMMENTARY: This chapter allows Holmes to display his famous deductive powers to the full. So far we have only seen flashes of Holmes at work but now we see him engaging in masterful analysis of fact and detail. Holmes is up early, ready, we feel, for action; the clients arrive punctually and we are immediately in the midst of a swiftly developing dialogue through which the plot is skilfully carried forward as we delight in Holmes's virtuoso performance. But before this begins we are provided with an introductory character sketch of Sir Henry. His physique, as it is described, suggests reliability and sturdy independence. Though his taste in clothing is certainly not good (it is implied that he has spent so much time out of doors that such matters do not concern him), he has, nevertheless, the manner of a gentleman; he is a man of good family, of dependable feelings and sound judgement. Quality, Conan Doyle is suggesting, will always show.

The strange message is examined. Conan Doyle chooses 'Charing Cross' as the place where the envelope was posted. Alert readers will remember that Charing Cross Hospital was where Dr Mortimer once worked and will begin to wonder, despite Mortimer's air of honesty, if he may be involved in some way with Sir Charles's death. Conan Doyle supplies this detail as a false clue to distract us a little from the main clue to the whole mystery, which this chapter provides in the story of the missing boot. At this stage in the tale the more threads that can be spun in the plot, some of them false threads, the less likely a reader is to unravel the whole mysterious affair before Conan Doyle wants him to, the more chance a reader's attention will be held through issue after issue of the *Strand Magazine*.

In the ensuing dialogue Holmes's is the dominant voice; he interrogates, directs the conversation, chooses the subjects to be discussed and with obvious enthusiasm exhibits his great skills as a sleuth. Conan Doyle provides him with opportunity after opportunity to do so:

1. He leaps to the brilliant conclusion that the strange message has been composed from words cut from an article in the previous day's edition of the London *Times*.
2. He displays his exact knowledge of newspaper type.
3. He deduces that the work was done with short-bladed scissors.
4. He estimates that the sender of the message is probably well-educated and that he has attempted to disguise this fact.
5. He concludes, through consideration of the penmanship, that the message was probably addressed from a hotel.
6. He notices something remarkable about the paper.

After this extraordinary performance, Conan Doyle introduces the matter of Sir Henry's boot, which of course is to be a crucial clue for Holmes. But instead of immediately grasping the implication of the boot's theft Conan Doyle has Holmes say 'It seems a singularly useless thing to steal ... I confess that I share Dr Mortimer's belief that it will not be long before the missing boot is found.' At this point Conan Doyle has managed to create complete faith in Holmes as a sleuth; so extraordinary have his powers of deduction appeared that Holmes's assessment of the missing boot as apparently irrelevant inclines us to ignore it. What we don't realise is that Holmes has his own good reasons for believing that the new unworn boot will soon turn up again. We imagine that it is because it has no relevance to the case and we press on to find out what happens next. So any chance of reflecting on the missing boot gets lost in Sir Henry's courageously determined declaration 'there is no man upon earth who can prevent me from going to the home of my own people' and in the exciting events with which the chapter concludes. But the chapter does not end without Holmes expressing himself on the case as a whole. Holmes seems deeply stirred at this point, disturbed by the solemnity and seriousness of the matter in hand. In a chapter where we have seen our hero so masterfully in action this admission is all the more effective, suggesting to us the extraordinary abilities of the opposition: 'We are dealing with a clever man, Watson. This matter cuts very deep ...'.

The chapter concludes with Holmes briskly setting about his investigations, arranging for a scrupulous, exhaustive search of hotel wastebaskets, letting us know that the enemy will have to reckon with not only Holmes's extraordinary powers of swift deduction but his dogged, persistent, inexhaustible attention to detail and his elevated calm which even at such a moment of high tension allows him a contemplative visit to a picture-gallery.

NOTES AND GLOSSARY
Times: *The Times* newspaper, probably the most famous English daily newspaper, which is published in London
leading articles: the daily editorials on topics of moment
supra-orbital crest, facial angle, maxillary curve: terms from Dr Mortimer's science
leaded bourgeois type: a kind and size of print
Leeds Mercury, Western Morning News: names of English provincial newspapers
cab: a horse-drawn carriage for hire
by wire: by telegraph wire

Chapter 5: Three Broken Threads

Holmes ascertains that no suspicious person is staying at the same hotel as Sir Henry. We learn that Sir Henry has lost a second boot, this time an old black one. Sir Henry declares that he still intends to go to Baskerville Hall and Holmes approves, informing him, however, that he is being followed in London. We learn that the butler at Baskerville Hall, Barrymore, has a full black beard, that he profited by the late Sir Charles's death and that he knew he would, as in fact did Dr Mortimer who also profited from the estate. The total value of the estate was, Mortimer tells us, 'close on to a million'. Mortimer provided information about the various claimants to the Baskerville inheritance. A telegram has been dispatched to Barrymore in Devon to check his presence there. It is decided that Holmes will stay in London for the present, that Watson will accompany Sir Henry to Devon and that he will report all important matters to Holmes. The new brown boot is discovered in Sir Henry's hotel-room and two telegrams arrive at Holmes's Baker Street home which provide no helpful information: Barrymore is at the Hall and the search of hotel waste-baskets in Charing Cross has unearthed no clue. The enquiries about the occupant of the London cab also draw a blank, though they do reveal that Holmes's antagonist knows of his interest in the case. Finally Watson prepares to go down to Devon with Holmes expressing forebodings about his safety there.

COMMENTARY: Up to this point in the book a reader might have been tempted to take the supernatural aspect of this tale rather seriously. Even in Chapter 4, thoughtful, scientific Dr Mortimer admitted that he hadn't made up his mind whether the death of Sir Charles is 'a case for a policeman or a clergyman' and a reader might be equally uncertain. Chapter 5, by contrast, serves to confirm a reader in his suspicion that the mystery has a perfectly natural explanation and that Holmes, through the exercise of his deductive powers, will unravel it. The chapter title itself, 'Three broken threads', suggests the threads of circumstance, fact and detail, which a careful sleuth must follow. Some will be broken threads but one will surely lead to the truth.

In this chapter, then, we see Holmes attending to detail after detail. Conan Doyle begins to surround the death of Sir Charles not with an atmosphere of supernatural horror but with details about the inheritance, about the value of the estate, about individuals who profited by the recent tragedy. We become aware of human motive as the possibility of supernatural agencies begins to fade in our minds. There is a sense of the author beginning to complicate the tale quite deliberately.

Barrymore is introduced more fully than in Chapter 2; he is equipped with the full black beard that casts suspicion on him and even apparently honest Dr Mortimer is made the recipient of a moderate sum as a result of Sir Charles's death. Then the enormous size of the estate suggests to us that many, all too human, beings might have had good cause to seek Sir Charles's untimely death.

Probably Conan Doyle knew it was necessary to complicate his tale at this point since Chapter 5 contains more information about Sir Henry's boots, the crucial clue in the book. But as this fact was treated confusingly in Chapter 4, so here it appears as simply one odd fact among many. Conan Doyle allows Dr Watson to summarise the events thus far in the novel, setting the strange business of the boots in the context of all the other strange events that have occurred. We are unlikely therefore to concentrate on the clue that could at the very least completely rule out supernatural explanations to the problem. 'Setting aside the whole grim story of Sir Charles's death, we had a line of inexplicable incidents all within the limits of two days, which included the receipt of the printed letter, the black-bearded spy in the hansom, the loss of the new brown boot, the loss of the old black boot, and now the return of the new brown boot.' Furthermore, at the very moment when Mortimer notices that his old black boot is missing, Conan Doyle has his characters take 'a pleasant luncheon in which little was said of the business which had brought us together'. A reader feels that even Holmes is at a loss. Conan Doyle makes Holmes assert again that this case is very difficult: 'When taken in conjunction with your uncle's death', he tells Sir Henry, 'I am not sure that of all the five hundred cases of capital importance which I have handled there is one that cuts so deep.' We assume that he feels at a loss, but at the end of the tale we understand that Holmes probably solved a good deal of the mystery in this chapter, for it is surely very obvious that a supernatural hound does not require the scent of its victims from shoes they have worn, and a detective of Holmes's experience must be credited with the ability to respond to a piece of fairly straightforward evidence. So what troubles him here is not the same thing that troubles us as readers. We are still led on by Watson's dull-witted incapacity to reach obvious conclusions; we are further convinced of the mysteriousness of the case by Holmes's assessment that it cuts deep: but by that he means he does not yet know how the criminal can be forced to reveal himself. We think he means that he is still *completely* in the dark, as we are, three broken threads in our hands.

In Chapter 5 Conan Doyle has (*i*) allowed us to consider the possibility of a criminal cause of death much more fully than before, and (*ii*) while providing Holmes with the evidence upon which he can base his subsequent actions, kept from us the facts: (*a*) that the boot is the crucial clue and (*b*) that Holmes must have deduced part of the truth about the case from the clue.

NOTES AND GLOSSARY
telegraph form: the form on which to write the contents of a telegram
caretaker: an individual whose job it is to protect a property in his charge
securities: stocks and bonds
public charities: organisations founded for charitable purposes, usually dependant on gifts and legacies
estate: property, fortune and possessions
a touch, Watson: an undeniable touch ... he got home ... a foil: three terms from the sport of fencing, signifying point-scoring
a toff: one who affects stylish superiority in manners and in attire
guinea: an English gold coin worth twenty-one shillings; now archaic

Chapter 6: Baskerville Hall

Holmes gives Watson his final instructions as the latter sets out for Devon. Holmes is certain of the innocence of Mr James Desmond, the next in line to inherit Baskerville Hall after Sir Henry. He also believes Dr Mortimer is uninvolved in the crime and asks Watson to pay attention to the people who live near Sir Henry on the moor. Holmes warns Sir Henry not to go about alone in Devon and makes certain Watson is armed. Watson and Sir Henry arrive in Devon where they hear of the escaped convict, Selden, who is loose on the moor. They arrive at Baskerville Hall and find it gloomy and intimidating. They are greeted by Mr and Mrs Barrymore. Barrymore informs Sir Henry that he and his wife wish to seek work elsewhere, and, despite Sir Henry's request that he reconsider, Barrymore remains firm in his decision. That night Watson, who cannot sleep, is disturbed by the sound of a woman sobbing.

COMMENTARY: An interesting feature of *The Hound of the Baskervi.* is that Sherlock Holmes is absent for much of the novel. Later reasoi will suggest why it was necessary for Holmes to allow Watson to take the centre of the stage for so much of the book. But this presented a severe problem to the author; how was he to shift readers' attentions away from the exciting figure of Holmes to the worthy but altogether less interesting figure of Watson without the reader feeling disappointed, perhaps a little cheated? This book after all represents the semi-return to life of the fabulous Sherlock Holmes and after allowing us five chapters in his company Conan Doyle took a considerable risk in banishing Holmes from the action until the very end of Chapter 11. Conan Doyle attempts to effect this transfer of interest from Holmes to Watson, without occasioning too much regret by two strategies.

Firstly our last glimpse of Holmes is of a powerful, mysterious, unforgettable figure. When Watson tells us 'I looked back at the platform when we had left it far behind and saw the tall, austere figure of Holmes standing motionless and gazing after us' it is a little difficult to believe that his commanding influence will not be felt in Devon; his presence will be felt despite his physical absence. As a result, a reader will probably feel that we are not leaving him behind at all.

Secondly Conan Doyle makes the very most he can of the Devonshire setting. So a reader, whilst he may be somewhat disappointed that Holmes is no longer physically present, feels that Watson and Sir Henry are travelling to a very interesting place indeed. Notice, for instance how the author drives home the point that Devonshire is a remarkable place and the moor, upon which Baskerville Hall is built, one of its chief wonders. Watson notes 'Young Baskerville stared eagerly out of the window, and cried aloud with delight as he recognised the familiar features of the Devon scenery'. Sir Henry is now 'young Baskerville'; the attractions of the landscape have released his youthful enthusiasm and, as Dr Mortimer implies, the Celtic strain in his temperament as well. We begin to share in Baskerville's excitable anticipation and Conan Doyle does not disappoint us, providing detailed descriptions of the moor, the house, indulging us with passages of atmospheric writing, satisfying a taste for romantic extravagance and for the gloom that pervades late eighteenth-century 'gothic' novels, or tales of terror. Even the worthy, dull Watson is imaginatively stirred in the ancestral dining hall of the ancient house:

> With rows of flaring torches to light it up, and the colour and rude hilarity of an old-time banquet, it might have softened; but now, when two black-clothed gentlemen sat in the little circle of light thrown by a shaded lamp, one's voice became hushed and one's spirit subdued. A dim line of ancestors, in every variety of dress, from the Elizabethan knight to the buck of the Regency stared down upon us and daunted us by their silent company.

28 · Summaries

But if all this is not enough to reconcile us to Holmes's absence, Conan Doyle provides us with further compensatory excitements:

(1) The threatening information about a violent murderer loose on the moor.
(2) Amidst such details as the chiming of a clock and the rustling of ivy at the 'very dead of night' (note the phrase familiar from a thousand tales of terror and the occult) 'the sob of a woman, the muffled, strangling gasp of one who is torn by an uncontrollable sorrow.'

By this point we have almost forgotten Sherlock Holmes.

NOTES AND GLOSSARY

first-class carriage: three classes of passenger carriage were originally provided on British railways, the first class being the most comfortable and expensive.
Celt, Gaelic, Ivernian: Celt, a person descended from the races who spoke one of the languages of the ancient Galli in Western Europe; Gaelic, Scottish and Irish Celtic; Ivernian, a variant of Hibernian, meaning Irish
cairns: heaps of stones raised in honour of the dead in prehistoric times
tors: high craggy hills
Swan and Edison: Sir Joseph Wilson Swan (1828–1914) and Thomas Alva Edison (1847–1931), inventors associated with the invention of electric light
minstrels' gallery: a balcony in a dining room where the musicians played during a banquet
Elizabethan knight: a gentleman honoured by a knighthood in the reign (1558–1603) of Elizabeth I (1533–1603) in English history
buck of the Regency: a dashing fellow, a dandy of the Regency period in English history. The Regency ran from 1811 to 1820, when the Prince Regent (1762–1830) became George IV
billiard-room: a room set apart for the playing of billiards, a game played with small hard balls on a cloth-covered table

Chapter 7: The Stapletons of Merripit House

By daylight Sir Henry and Watson feel more at home in Baskerville Hall, though Sir Henry has also been disturbed in the night by the mysterious sobbing. They question Barrymore on this matter and he assures them that it was not his wife they heard. After breakfast Watson chances upon Mrs Barrymore whose red eyes and swollen lids betray Barrymore's lie. Watson determines to establish whether the test telegram sent from London had actually been received by Barrymore in person. Watson walks the four miles to ask the village postmaster about this. His enquiries reveal that the telegram was delivered to Mrs Barrymore because Barrymore was in the loft. As Watson ponders this fact he is interrupted by a stranger, who turns out to be a friend of Dr Mortimer, Mr Stapleton of Merripit House, a local naturalist. Stapleton talks of the manner of Sir Charles's death, proposing his theory that the dead man did in fact see a dog on the moor and, since his heart was weak, died of fright. Stapleton reveals that he is aware of Sherlock Holmes's interest in the case. Watson denies this. Watson accepts Stapleton's invitation to visit his home. They walk there past the Great Grimpen Mire where they see a donkey perishing horribly. Stapleton warns Watson of the extreme danger of the place. They hear the strange long, low moan which Stapleton identifies as the sound the peasants believe to be the Hound of the Baskervilles. Stapleton suggests natural explanations for the mysterious sound. While Stapleton chases a fly or moth Watson is met by Miss Stapleton, the naturalist's sister, who orders him back to London, though gives no explanation for her behaviour. Miss Stapleton hides from her brother the fact that she has advised Watson to return to London, and in their home Watson learns of Stapleton's career as a failed schoolmaster and of his current scientific interests. Stapleton wishes to visit Sir Henry in the afternoon. Watson returns to Baskerville Hall. On the way he is met by Miss Stapleton who has taken a short cut to inform Watson that she had mistaken him for Sir Henry. She believes, it transpires, in the legend of the hound and fears for Sir Henry's safety.

COMMENTARY: Conan Doyle must have found this a very difficult chapter to write. In it he must introduce us to the book's villain, Stapleton. He must solve the delicate problem of presenting a character upon whom suspicion can reasonably fall, but without making that character's villainy transparently obvious. As in earlier chapters when Conan Doyle wished to distract us from the lost boots he provided other matters to engage our attention, so in this chapter he allows most suspicion to be directed at the Barrymores rather than at Stapleton. Although Stapleton could, in view of his manner and conversation, properly be the main object of our suspicions at this point, we tend to suspect the Barrymores rather more. Conan Doyle makes us more suspicious of the Barrymores than of Stapleton in several ways:

(1) The pale-faced, black-bearded Barrymore is set against the fresh beauty of the morning, making him seem all the more possibly a villain, whereas we are introduced to Stapleton in the context of extended descriptions of the fearsome landscape. Our attention is divided between the character and the landscape. Barrymore had stood out clearly as a possible villain against the description of a sunny morning. Stapleton may be as evil as the landscape in which we first see him but our divided attention is unlikely to allow us to come to a quick decision about this.

(2) Barrymore is quite bluntly portrayed as a liar and we meet Stapleton with this fact to the fore in our minds. It is why Barrymore lied and why his wife wept that we wish to discover, not why Stapleton converses so suspiciously.

(3) By contrast with the suspicion that must surround Barrymore after his bare-faced lie and his possible trick over the telegram, the suspicion that surrounds Stapleton is the less, since it is based on the much more subtle fact that Miss Stapleton does not wish her brother to know that she has warned Watson (whom she believes is Sir Henry) to flee from Devonshire.

(4) Watson himself spends time pondering the question of a motive for Barrymore. At this stage he ignores Stapleton.

Conan Doyle, with Watson as his tool, is cleverly using the Barrymores to distract us from the true villain. This he continues to do in subsequent chapters.

Stapleton's conversation is very cleverly managed. We cannot tell whether his rather nervous, knowing manner is evidence of innocence or guilt. He clearly wants to meet Sir Henry and is very anxious to hear about Sir Henry's attitude to the Baskerville curse. He seems almost guiltily concerned to propound a believable theory about Sir Charles's death which might, to an attentive reader, suggest his guilt. We learn too that he knew of Sir Charles's heart condition and that he is very much interested as to whether Sherlock Holmes is to come to Devonshire. There is perhaps nothing damning about all of this, nor in the fact that he, as a recent inhabitant of Devon (he has lived there for only two years), can penetrate the Grimpen Mire (he may after all as an enthusiastic naturalist have wished to search for rare species there) but it may add up to something that a reader should notice and remember.

Watson, of course, doesn't seem to notice these things at all. He is more concerned to question Stapleton about the mysterious sound they hear and about the prehistoric past of the moor. His earnest failure to suspect Stapleton influences us, even when Miss Stapleton provides her lame explanation for her odd behaviour.

At the end of the chapter Watson heads back to Baskerville Hall, his 'soul full of vague fears'. He needs Sherlock Holmes, as we do too, to get to the bottom of this mystery.

NOTES AND GLOSSARY
coats-of-arms: heraldic devices on shields peculiar to a particular man or family
granite: a hard igneous rock
bittern booming: the bittern is a bird (now rare in Britain) known for its booming cry
wigwams: primitive dwelling-houses
Neolithic man: early man from the Neolithic period of tool-making and farming
Cyclopides, Lepidoptera: kinds of butterflies and moths

Chapter 8: First Report of Dr Watson

Watson decides that he can best inform us about subsequent events in Devon by allowing us to read his correspondence to Holmes directed, as he thought at the time, to the detective in London. In the first letter Watson reports on his feelings for the Devonshire landscape with its sense of prehistoric antiquity, and he recounts the latest news of the escaped murderer who appears to have fled the country. He describes the Stapleton household and informs Holmes that Sir Henry appears to have fallen in love with Miss Stapleton. Watson has met Mortimer again, and has encountered another of the local inhabitants of the moor, Mr Frankland of Lafter Hall, who is passionately interested in the Law. In Watson's opinion his most interesting news concerns the Barrymores. Sir Henry has asked Barrymore directly if he received Holmes's telegram into his own hands. His reply confirms the postmaster's earlier account of events—his wife brought it up to him in the loft. Barrymore is concerned that Sir Henry no longer has confidence in him. The chapter ends with Watson revealing his most extraordinary information. The night before Watson wrote this report to Holmes he was wakened by Barrymore prowling about the house and Watson rose, followed him and observed the man peering in obvious mental anguish out over the moor. Watson then tells Holmes that he and Sir Henry have decided upon a plan of action.

32 · Summaries

COMMENTARY: Just as we seriously begin to regret Sherlock Holmes's absence from the scene, Conan Doyle has the good sense to bring him some way back into his novel by the simple ploy of having Watson write to him. The slow, almost ponderous style Watson employs as a letter-writer is worth considering. We are now mid-way through the story. In the last two chapters we have been very conscious, in the extended descriptions of landscape and locale, of the possible supernatural influences on human actions. The moor is so mysterious, so powerful in its brooding otherworldliness that Watson is still wondering with troubled anxiety as he thinks in this chapter of Sir Charles's last moments—'There was the long, gloomy tunnel down which he fled. And from what? A sheep-dog on the moor? Or a spectral hound, black, silent, and monstrous? Was there a human agency in the matter?' We too, as readers, have become affected by the moor's strange presences and have perhaps begun to wonder with Watson if Sir Charles's death was a supernatural event. So we welcome Watson's painstaking, slow setting down of the facts as he has discovered them. We can imagine Holmes (for we, like Watson, think he is in London) sifting through the details as they come to him, piecing them into a coherent natural order. The book therefore seems poised at a moment where we have learnt much, yet we still remain confused. We read on in anticipation of future clarifying revelations, welcoming a chance to gather our wits.

The reader will notice that Watson is still concentrating on the Barrymores, scarcely troubling to consider Stapleton as a possible villain, despite his awareness of the man's 'positive and possibly... harsh nature'. Conan Doyle, through Watson, is still firmly leading us exactly where he wants us to go: to Barrymore alone before a night window, staring 'out into the blackness of the moor'.

NOTES AND GLOSSARY
monolith: a pillar of stone, often shaped into a monument
groom: a servant in charge of horses
tête-a-tête: (*French*) an intimate conversation between two people

Chapter 9: Second Report of Dr Watson

In this second report from Watson to Holmes, Watson informs the sleuth that he has ascertained that Barrymore has apparently been contacting someone on the moor by night. Watson has informed Sir Henry, who has also heard the servant up and about at night. Watson suspects Barrymore of a love intrigue which might account for his wife's weeping. They are determined to follow him another night to find out why he is behaving so strangely. Watson reports on Sir Henry's developing romance with Miss Stapleton. He tells how he followed Sir Henry on to the moor lest he should come to harm. There Sir Henry and Miss Stapleton met. He tells Holmes of Stapleton's extraordinary displeasure at the lovers' meeting. Sir Henry is very confused by Stapleton's reaction to a possible marriage between his sister and himself. Miss Stapleton has, we learn, contrived to urge Sir Henry's departure from Devonshire. Watson can think of no good reason why Stapleton should object to so fortunate a match for his sister. However, that very afternoon Stapleton came to apologise to Sir Henry and the quarrel is apparently mended. Sir Henry is to dine at Stapleton's house on the coming Friday. Stapleton is so attached to his sister, according to his testimony to Sir Henry, that he cannot bear to think of her marriage. He has asked Sir Henry to let the matter rest for three months and Sir Henry has agreed.

Watson then reports on developments in the matter of Barrymore's suspicious activity. On the second night, lying in wait for the butler, Watson and Sir Henry have confronted Barrymore as he made his mysterious journey about the house in the middle of the night. Watson guessed that the butler was signalling to someone on the moor. Afterwards, by signalling from the window with a candle, Watson observed an answering light on the moor. Sir Henry demanded an explanation which Mrs Barrymore provided. Selden, the escaped convict hiding on the moor, is her brother. The Barrymores had been sending him food on those occasions when their signal had met with an answer from the moor. Sir Henry then determined to capture the convict and Watson and he set out across the moor, where Watson reports they heard the strange hound-like cry again. They came upon Selden but the convict, alerted to their arrival at his hiding place, escaped them. Watson ends his report to Holmes by recounting how, just when they had decided to abandon their pursuit of Selden, they saw a strange man, standing on an outcrop of rock, silhouetted against the moon.

COMMENTARY: In this chapter Stapleton begins to behave in a very suspicious manner. Even Watson finds it difficult to ignore the man's eccentricities of behaviour and the violence of his feelings. However, Watson is so intent on letting Holmes know of the unmasking of the Barrymores that he doesn't stop to ponder the significance of Stapleton's insistence on the postponement of his sister's engagement to Sir Henry. He takes Stapleton's apologetic excuse for his emotional outburst at its face value, even feeling a certain stolid pride in his own deductive abilities: 'So there is one of our small mysteries cleared up. It is something to have touched bottom anywhere in this bog in which we

34 · Summaries

are floundering. We know now why Stapleton looked with disfavour upon his sister's suitor—even when that suitor was so eligible a one as Sir Henry'. He doesn't, of course, as we suspect and later discover. In unmasking the Barrymores Watson takes a special pride, not apparently realising that in discovering the truth about their activities he has reached the end of a broken thread in his investigations. Since the Barrymores were merely catering to the needs of Selden, they were not at this point engaging in acts that would connect them with Sir Charles's death, because Selden escaped from prison some time after that event. As readers we feel that little has been clarified, that the mystery remains as great despite Watson's dogged persistence. We begin to wish with a little irritation that Holmes would arrive to reveal all. Watson cannot tell when he has come to the end of a broken thread, but Conan Doyle knew that his readers would probably not be so dim-witted. They might well experience disappointment when they realise that they have been led down a road that goes nowhere. At this point the author must give them something to quicken their excitement immediately, to take them across what might have seemed an odd gap in the narrative. Conan Doyle does this in two ways:

(1) He allows the hound to bay yet again, reminding us of the real object of Holmes's enquiries. Conan Doyle is concerned here to evoke the horrible cry as frighteningly as possible. He makes the sound really 'strident, wild and menacing', arresting our attention.

(2) He stimulates our interest anew by introducing a further element in the plot to replace the mystery surrounding the Barrymores: we see the mysterious figure against the moon.

NOTES AND GLOSSARY
butterfly net: a net used to capture butterflies and moths
prairie: a wide grassland
straight-jacket: a strong tight jacket for restraining the violently insane or criminal
hunting-crop: a stiff whip for urging on a horse in the hunt
peat: soft vegetable tissue formed by the partial decomposition of plants in water; it covers many of the moors of the British Isles

---

Chapter 10: Extract from the Diary of Dr Watson

Dr Watson now allows us to read extracts from the diary he kept whilst in Devonshire with Sir Henry. The first extract begins on the morning after the unsuccessful attempt to capture Selden. In this he reflects on the possible explanations of the mystery and ponders the facts established thus far. Watson determines to discover the identity of the stranger observed the night before. Watson then records in his diary the fact that Barrymore has complained of his master hunting Selden down when it was he who provided information about the unfortunate convict's presence on the moor. He has persuaded Sir Henry and Dr Watson to allow Selden to escape to South America unhindered. To express his gratitude Barrymore has revealed that when Sir Charles died the baronet was at the gate waiting for a woman, whose initials he knows were L.L. Barrymore's wife discovered the charred remains of this letter in the fireplace of Sir Charles's study. The letter made an appointment with Sir Charles for the evening on which he died. Watson and Sir Henry decide to make efforts to discover the identity of L.L. The next day's entry in Watson's diary describes a walk the doctor took on the moor in rainy weather. He met Dr Mortimer who gave him a lift home in his dog-cart. Dr Mortimer knows of a woman in Coombe Tracey, from where the mysterious letter was sent, whose initials are L.L. She is Laura Lyons, the daughter of Mr Frankland, the eccentric with a passion for the Law. She has married unfortunately. Her husband, an artist named Lyons, has deserted her, and with the help of a few of the Devonshire people, including Stapleton and Sir Charles, she has started a typewriting business. Dr Watson decides he will visit Mrs Lyons and seek further information.

In his diary Watson records a further incident of October 17th. After dinner he questioned Barrymore on Selden's movements. It emerges, in this conversation, that Barrymore knows of the strange man on the moor. Selden has told Barrymore about this and Barrymore finds it disturbing. He is very afraid for Sir Henry. Watson further questioned the butler about the stranger who, it seems, is 'a kind of gentleman' whose food is brought to his hideout in the huts on a hillside by a lad who works for him. Watson reflects anxiously on this man's identity.

COMMENTARY: Suspicion is now clearly directed towards the unknown stranger, though the plot is further complicated by the new information about Sir Charles's reason for being out of doors on the night of his death. However, despite these two new details in the developing tale the basic elements of the book established in earlier chapters are merely consolidated in this chapter. They are:

(1) The moor as an area of atmospheric mystery.
(2) The possibility that the hound may have a supernatural origin.
(3) Holmes as a master of deduction from facts and Watson as an earnest, worthy observer of facts he cannot interpret correctly.

In this chapter Stapleton is kept very much in the background. Indeed Conan Doyle uses Selden, the escaped convict, to make Stapleton seem momentarily vulnerable and probably innocent. Watson, at Conan Doyle's direction, thinks of Stapleton as a possible victim of Selden's criminality which tends to reduce any unfavourable impression he may have made on us earlier since:

(1) Watson clearly has no idea he is the villain.
(2) It is difficult to think of him as a criminal in face of the portrait of horrendous criminality which Selden represents.

NOTES AND GLOSSARY
dog-cart: a light, one-horse carriage
écarté: (*French*) a card game for two persons

Chapter 11: The Man on the Tor

Watson returns to a straightforward recounting of the events as he remembers them. Watson decides to confront Mrs Lyons on his own. After an initial refusal she agrees to answer Watson's questions. She tells him that it was through Stapleton that Sir Charles heard about her difficult matrimonial and financial situation. At first she denies having written to Sir Charles on the day of his death, but confronted with the evidence she admits the truth. Yet she very forcibly denies that she kept her appointment with Sir Charles on the fatal evening. Mrs Lyons tells Watson that the contents of her letter to Sir Charles were very private, a request for help in seeking her freedom through legal separation from her husband. She did not keep the appointment because help was made available to her from another source in the interval. Watson believes she is largely telling the truth, but has doubts of her innocence nevertheless. He determines to search the hiding-place of the strange man on the moor.

In this he is aided by Mr Frankland, whom he meets by chance as he is returning from his visit to Coombe Tracey. Frankland invites him into his home. In the midst of boring tales of his legal successes he lets slip that he thinks he knows where the convict on the moor is hiding. Frankland thinks that the convict's food is brought to him each day by a child. Watson, having private knowledge about Selden, immediately realises that Frankland has discovered the whereabouts not of Selden, but of the mysterious stranger. Frankland tells Watson that the child goes each day to a hill on the stoniest part of the moor. Indeed, at that moment Frankland observes the child and allows Watson to use his telescope to inspect him in more detail. Watson leaves Frankland's home and sets off, although it is already getting late, in hope of discovering the mysterious stranger's identity. He finds the man's hiding place and in it a sheet of paper on which some writing refers, very surprisingly, to himself. Watson concludes that it is he and not Sir Henry who is being followed by the unknown man. He patiently sits down to wait for his arrival. At last the stranger returns to his hiding-place and addresses the Doctor in a voice that both he and we recognise with a flood of relief.

COMMENTARY: The last three chapters, while exciting enough at times, have been somewhat slower paced than the earlier chapters of the book. Conan Doyle has used Dr Watson's rather ponderously compiled reports and diary entries to slow down the pace of the book's action, to allow for a section of the work in which the plot is made more complicated by the introduction of new characters and in which the atmospheric possibilities of the moor are exploited to the full. It would have been difficult to maintain the rather hectic speed of earlier chapters right through the book and readers might even have found it exhausting if the author had. So we have been allowed a kind of interlude. By now, though, we want the action to proceed; like Watson himself, we are becoming somewhat impatient at the way the mystery keeps deepening; we are still disappointed that the Barrymore plot has led to nothing. Like Watson, we wish things would begin to clarify. Conan Doyle, through Watson, at this very moment promises that they will. Watson tells us that the next few days contained crucial events, so 'indelibly graven upon my recollection, . . . I can tell them without reference to the notes made at the time'. So, in this chapter, we realise that we are beginning to read about the final stages of the Doctor's adventures in Devonshire (remember a reader of the story in its original serial form could not, as we can, easily determine how far on in the action he was simply by looking at the page number). Interest quickens anew just at the point where it might have begun to slacken as Conan Doyle ends the chapter with the altogether surprising revelation that the mysterious man on the moor is Sherlock Holmes and has been all the time. With this shock foremost in our minds we are unlikely to remember that this is the chapter where we learn that Stapleton had acted as an inter-mediary between Mrs Lyons and Sir Charles. We perhaps fail to note that this is a detail which might reasonably cause great suspicion to fall upon him. Conan Doyle is still keeping us agreeably in suspense.

NOTES AND GLOSSARY

almoner: one who dispenses alms or charity on behalf of someone else

trap:	a light, usually two-wheel, horse-drawn carriage
magnate:	a person of distinction or rank, a noble
commoners:	the common people
pannikin:	a small pan or cup
Spartan habits:	habits of fortitude in great physical endurance; from the people of Sparta, famed in ancient times for their military valour and endurance.

Chapter 12: Death on the Moor

Watson greets Holmes with great enthusiasm. Holmes is also aware of Mrs Lyons's involvement in the mystery. He explains to Watson why he has deceived his friend, allowing him to believe he was in London when in fact he has been in Devonshire all the time. It was for his own protection and to enable Holmes to investigate the case undetected. Watson is placated by Holmes's warm praise of his reports which have been forwarded to him in his hideout. Watson tells Holmes of his visit to Mrs Lyons. The detective is deeply interested. Holmes reveals that an intimacy exists between Mrs Lyons and Stapleton and that the lady who passes for Stapleton's sister is in fact his wife. So Watson at last realises that Stapleton must be the prime suspect in the case. Watson's information about Mrs Lyons wishing to institute divorce proceedings supplies Holmes with an explanation for her part in the matter—she hoped to become Stapleton's wife. Holmes believes that the truth about the villain will be a powerful weapon to use against Mrs Lyons in persuading her to reveal all she knows and he determines to visit her the next day. Holmes warns Watson that Sir Henry is in danger and that the case they are investigating is one of murder.

Suddenly the two men are interrupted by a frightful scream, and as they rush out into the darkness they hear the sound of the great hound. They struggle across the moor in pursuit of the frightening sounds. Holmes is in great anguish of mind fearing that through his risking Sir Henry's life he may be partly responsible for his death. They come upon a body which they recognise as Sir Henry's by the tweed suit they know to be his. He has apparently died from a fall. As they decide to send for help in removing the body Holmes realises that the dead man is not in fact Sir Henry but Selden, the criminal. Barrymore, Watson remembers, had passed on Sir Henry's old clothes to his convict brother-in-law to help him in his escape and the hound, alerted to Sir Henry's scent by the boot stolen from the hotel, has followed and killed the unfortunate criminal who, attired in another man's suit, is an accidental victim of Stapleton's villainy. Holmes cannot understand why Selden's body is so contorted with fear at the baying of the hound, while Watson is anxious to know why the hound was loose on the moor that night. Does Stapleton believe Sir Henry is on the moor? At this moment Stapleton appears, pretends shock at Sir Henry's death, and is genuinely shocked to learn that Selden is the dead man. Stapleton informs them that he is on the moor in concern for Sir Henry whom he had invited over to his house. Stapleton is anxious to know if Watson and Holmes heard anything else but the convict's cry as he fell to his death. Holmes replies that they did not and Watson tells Stapleton, to his evident relief, that he believes Selden died in an accident. He was deranged by exposure to the elements and died in a fall. Stapleton enquires if Sherlock Holmes agrees with this conclusion, revealing that he recognises the detective. Holmes assures Stapleton that Watson's explanation will cover the facts and informs him that he intends to return to London the next day. Holmes and Watson set off to Baskerville Hall wondering how they are to prove their case against Stapleton. Holmes is confident that Mrs Lyons will give them a lead when they confront her. Holmes decides that the next day, when Sir Henry goes to dine with the Stapletons, he must go alone, in ignorance of Selden's death and of how it occurred.

COMMENTARY: With Holmes back at the centre of the stage, events follow thick and fast. At last Watson, and the reader, realise that Stapleton is the villain as everything begins to come clear. In this chapter we learn that: (1) Holmes has been in Devonshire throughout; (2) there is a liaison between Stapleton and Mrs Lyons; (3) Stapleton's sister is in fact his wife, and (4) Stapleton is obviously the villain. So it is at this point that a reader finally accepts that Sir Charles was murdered and that his death was not the result of some supernatural event. He knows too that Stapleton is the book's villain. With so much being revealed so quickly a reader might feel some disappointment, as if he has suddenly grasped how a conjuring trick has been performed. Conan Doyle, perhaps aware of this, provides the reader with a great deal to engage his attention in this chapter. Any disappointment he may have felt that the mystery has been so easily solved is forgotten in the swiftly moving account of Selden's death and in the shift of attention away from the question of the villain's identity to the gripping problem as to how Holmes will trap him and prove his guilt. It is that which now keeps us reading.

NOTES AND GLOSSARY
lintel: the horizontal beam over a door (or window)
gorse bushes: prickly yellow-flowered bushes found on moorland

Chapter 13: Fixing the Nets

Watson breaks the news of Selden's death to the Barrymores. Sir Henry reports that he had received an invitation for the evening from Stapleton but that he had declined it. Holmes notices the portraits of the Baskerville family in the Hall and realises that one bears a striking resemblance to Stapleton, thereby deducing that the man is a Baskerville with designs upon the succession. Next day Holmes tells Sir Henry that Watson and he are returning to London and that he must venture to Stapleton's house alone that evening. Sir Henry, despite misgivings, agrees to obey Holmes even to the detail of letting Stapleton know that he intends to walk home across the moor. Holmes orders him to keep very strictly to the straight path from Merripit House. Holmes and Watson then travel to Coombe Tracey to interview Mrs Lyons. On the way Holmes arranges for a message to go to Sir Henry confirming with him that they have gone to London. Holmes receives a telegram informing him of the imminent arrival of a Scotland Yard policeman with an unsigned warrant.

Holmes informs Mrs Lyons of Stapleton's married state. Realising this she confesses that it was Stapleton who dictated the contents of her letter to Sir Charles and that he then dissuaded her from keeping the appointment. She has since kept silent for fear of being implicated in a crime and in hope of marriage to Stapleton. Holmes and Watson leave to meet the London train which carried Lestrade, the policeman, to Devonshire.

COMMENTARY: We now know Stapleton's motive and have learnt of his relationship to Sir Henry. The mystery is almost entirely solved. All that remains in doubt is the means by which Stapleton killed Sir Charles. The excitement is generated now, not by our desire to get at the truth, but by our anxiety to know if Holmes's elaborately laid trap for the villain will succeed.

NOTES AND GLOSSARY
warrant: a document issued by a magistrate authorising a police officer to make an arrest

Chapter 14: The Hound of the Baskervilles

Holmes, Watson and Lestrade return to the moor where they hide near Stapleton's house to await events. Watson creeps up to the house where he observes Stapleton and Sir Henry through a window but does not see Mrs Stapleton. Fog begins to drift across the moor from the Grimpen Mire. It is thickening as they hear Sir Henry walk past them in the darkness. Then, out of the fog, appears the devilish hound, fire bursting from its mouth. They give chase and Holmes wounds the animal with a pistol-shot. As it leaps to the kill Holmes dispatches it with five bullets. Sir Henry is unharmed. The hound had been coated with phosphorous to make it a fearsome, ghastly brute. Holmes and Watson rush back to Merripit House where they discover Mrs Stapleton bound and gagged. Stapleton has fled. She, highly relieved that Sir Henry is safe and the hound dead, tells them that her husband has probably fled to an old tin mine in the heart of the Mire where he had housed the great hound while waiting for his chance to murder Sir Henry. Holmes and Watson, with Sir Henry, go to the Hall where the baronet is informed of Mrs Stapleton's true marital state. Sir Henry is greatly distressed and this news, together with the shock of the evening's events, brings on a delirious fever.

Next day Mrs Stapleton guides Holmes and Watson through the Mire, where they come upon Sir Henry's missing boot. They find no trace of the villain, only remnants of the food he had given his murderous hound. It is assumed that Stapleton perished in the Mire.

COMMENTARY: The hound runs. Sir Henry is saved, despite the fog. Holmes has won but at the expense of Sir Henry's health. The mood of the chapter is more troubled than triumphant, suggesting perhaps that the Great Mire and the moor have the final victory.

Chapter 15: A Retrospection

Holmes in retrospect ties up all the remaining threads of the mystery and summarises the case, lest we have missed anything of significance. Stapleton was in fact the son of Rodger Baskerville who many years before fled to South America. Stapleton had returned to England fairly recently, deciding then to murder Sir Henry and to acquire his valuable estate.

COMMENTARY: In this chapter Stapleton's full villainy is made apparent. He was a systematic, cold-blooded criminal, responsible for many robberies. His last plot went astray because of Holmes's brilliant intervention. Later we must ask ourselves how convincing Holmes's explanations are in this chapter. At this point it is enough to take our leave of Watson and Holmes, mingling our regret with a sense of pleasure at the way so many details of the plot have brought us to this moment of completion and satisfying retrospection.

Part 3

Commentary

Introduction

In criticising a work of literature it is always necessary to know what kind of a work is being considered. It is pointless to criticise a comic tale for a lack of high seriousness, if high seriousness was no part of the author's intention. So in assessing the merits of *The Hound of the Baskervilles* the reader must always keep clearly in mind what kind of a work the author meant it to be. In Part 1 of this study we saw that Conan Doyle intended his Sherlock Holmes tales for a mass audience and that he had no very great aesthetic and artistic ambitions for them. He reserved artistic seriousness for his much less successful historical romances. In tales like *The Hound of the Baskervilles* he hoped to entertain his audience rather than instruct, inspire, warn or criticise it. So the Sherlock Holmes tales might more properly be described as entertainments than as works of serious literature. It is as such that we must assess *The Hound of the Baskervilles*. But in thinking about the book as an entertainment the reader should beware of condescending to the form. The ability to entertain should not be undervalued.

The specific literary form of *The Hound of the Baskervilles*

In *The Hound of the Baskervilles* Conan Doyle combines two kinds of tale: (*i*) The detective story and (*ii*) The tale of the supernatural.
    Writing about a detective allowed Conan Doyle to cater to an audience's need for a particular kind of hero. (See p.9) The detective story form also allowed Conan Doyle to entertain excitingly. He used the form to write brisk, absorbing adventure stories where the element of detection is simply part of the exciting world of action he portrays. In this he breaks with the tradition of detective fiction as he knew it.
    English detective fiction is usually thought to originate with Wilkie Collins's book *The Moonstone* (1867) with its detective, Sergeant Cuff. Before that, between the years 1840 and 1845, the American poet and short-story writer Edgar Allan Poe wrote *The Murders in the Rue*

Morgue, *The Purloined Letter*, and *The Mystery of Marie Roget* in which a detective named Dupin engages in amazing feats of systematic analysis in solving criminal cases. (*The Mystery of Marie Roget* was based on actual occurrences). In Poe and Wilkie Collins a reader may find the groundwork being laid for the development of the detective story as a distinct literary form. Both writers present us with puzzling examples of crime and with a detective who solves the puzzle through the exercise of his deductive powers. From Wilkie Collins Conan Doyle probably learnt that the figure of the detective must be sympathetically treated, he must be a personality. Sergeant Cuff is a human being in *The Moonstone*, not simply an analytic reasoning machine as Dupin is in Poe's stories. From *The Moonstone* Conan Doyle may also have learnt of the usefulness of atmosphere in detective fiction, for the book has its passages of hair-raising sensation. From Poe, Conan Doyle probably learnt how important systematic deduction can be in a detective story. However, Conan Doyle placed more emphasis on action than detection in his stories. In this way he succeeded in making them more entertaining than Poe's pioneering efforts. Poe used the detective story form to make a serious point about the relationship of knowledge to scientific evidence. In Poe we are offered tedious masses of fact and detail as if the tale is a metaphor of pure reason at work in the world untangling a web of ambiguities and mystery. In Conan Doyle's work, and *The Hound of the Baskervilles* is typical in this respect, the detection is treated as an exciting, perhaps frightening puzzle which leads the main characters into dangerous adventures before the mystery is at last clarified. The reader is allowed the pleasure of pondering the work as a puzzle but not to such a degree that the work becomes a serious study of the nature of evidence. The swift-moving action prevents that, keeping the entertainment level high.

In the twentieth century the detective story form has been refined and polished by many expert practitioners until it has become a highly conventional kind of work which must obey a series of complicated rules. Interested readers may find these rules outlined in H. Douglas Thomas's *Masters of Mystery: A Study of the Detective Story* (1931).

Conan Doyle's stories, written when the form was in its infancy, do not have the classical purity of some later examples in the mode (by later standards he breaks rules and is careless with details of setting; it would be an unfortunate reader who took *The Hound of the Baskervilles* as an accurate guide to the geography, topography and ecology of Devonshire). But while his stories may be faulted by the purist, he must be assured a place in the history of detective fiction for two reasons: (*i*) He saw the potentialities of employing two central characters (the detective and a loyal companion) and (*ii*) His stories with their vivid main characters are entertaining and thrilling.

The supernatural tale or tale of the uncanny serves as an entertainment if it frightens us pleasurably, though occasionally, as with the detective story, the form has been used to do more than entertain. Henry James's *The Turn of the Screw* (1898), for example, achieves a note of genuine tragedy absent from most stories of this kind. The supernatural tale, which became really popular in the late eighteenth and in the nineteenth centuries, as traditional religious beliefs about the after-life were increasingly subjected to rational scepticism, seeks to disturb us out of a daylight common-sense view of the world by playing upon our fears of darkness, death, sickness, fate, the primitive and the irrational. Such tales succeed as entertainments when their sensationalism and mastery of atmosphere create pleasurable rather than unpleasant apprehension. The apparently supernatural hound in *The Hound of the Baskervilles* has just such an effect. Perhaps the idea of a family haunted by an ancient curse in the shape of a supernatural hound is almost too gothic to be taken seriously, but at moments in the book (and you must list them carefully) a reader's skin crawls with a curiously enjoyable horror.

SUMMARY: (*i*) *The Hound of the Baskervilles* was written to entertain and must be judged with this in mind; (*ii*) in *The Hound of the Baskervilles* Conan Doyle combines the detective tale with the tale of the supernatural; (*iii*) Conan Doyle underplays the detection in his detective tale, substituting exciting action. The book is therefore highly entertaining and Conan Doyle uses the supernatural to create pleasurable and entertaining sensations of fear.

Suggested themes

While *The Hound of the Baskervilles* is an entertainment, it is not simply a clever detective story in which a popular hero undergoes a series of skilfully plotted adventures, nor is it simply a sensationalist exploitation of supernatural horrors for their own sake. Indeed, what makes it so effective as an entertainment is that the book contains suggestions of serious themes imaginatively treated. So a reader, enjoying the clever portrayals of Holmes and Watson at work, pondering the puzzle-like mystery, relishing the swift-moving plot, can congratulate himself that he is not merely indulging in a taste for undemanding entertainment but that he is attending to a work of some artistic importance. The reader's imagination, as well as his intellect and emotions, can be involved in the book. The following serious themes are suggested by the book's narrative.

The countryside and the city

A reader has a strong sense in the book that the city is the natural environment for a man of Holmes's intellectual powers. He seems at ease there, working in his Baker Street flat, attending an art gallery, checking the times of trains, calling a hansom cab. On the Devonshire moor he is much less self-assured, even at moments capable of anguished self-doubt. On the moor the masterful Sherlock Holmes admits, when he thinks Sir Henry has been destroyed by the hound, 'I am more to blame than you, Watson. In order to have my case well rounded and complete, I have thrown away the life of my client. It is the greatest blow which has befallen me in my career. But how could I know—how *could* I know—that he would risk his life alone upon the moor in face of all my warnings.' The moor is a place where even Holmes's great intellectual powers seem to falter, where his plans and stratagems have to contend with chance and unpredictable natural forces. Indeed at the very end of the tale Holmes's plans almost go astray since he had not bargained for the thick fog which settles over the moor. In the country Holmes seems a much less formidable, more vulnerable figure than he does in London. The moor itself is a powerful and worthy adversary. So the contrast between Holmes in London and in Devonshire suggests a conflict between urban intelligence and the darker forces of nature, unpredictable and ungovernable.

Science and the supernatural

Conan Doyle uses the supernatural to maintain suspense in the book. For a long time he allows us to wonder whether Holmes is facing a supernatural rather than a human enemy. The effect of this is not simply to create suspense but to suggest a conflict, related to the contrast between the city and the country, between the man of science and the powers of darkness. The moor and especially Grimpen Mire begin to take on symbolic value in the book, as they are associated with the prehistoric, the ancient, the wild, with all that can overpower the life of the mind, dragging it down into the destructive depths of fear and irrationality. So Dr Watson tells Miss Stapleton 'Life has become like that great Grimpen Mire, with little green patches everywhere into which one may sink and with no guide to point the track.' When Watson accompanies the baronet and Stapleton to see the spot where the legend of the wicked Hugo was supposed to have had its origin he finds:

> It was an excursion of some miles across the moor to a place which is so dismal that it might have suggested the story. We found a short valley between rugged tors which led to an open, grassy space flecked over with the white cotton grass. In the middle of it rose two great stones, worn and sharpened at the upper end, until they looked like the huge corroding fangs of some monstrous beast. In every way it corresponded with the scene of the old tragedy.

Notice that the landscape itself reminds the reader of the hound of the Baskervilles. (The 'two great stones' resemble the 'fangs of some monstrous beast'). Later in his journal Watson tells us of his walk on the lonely moor, in a passage where the symbolic possibilities of the Great Mire are present to powerful effect:

> In the evening I put on my waterproof and I walked far upon the sodden moor, full of dark imaginings, the rain beating upon my face and the wind whistling about my ears. God help those who wander into the Great Mire now, for even the firm uplands are becoming a morass. I found the Black Tor upon which I had seen the solitary watcher, and from its craggy summit I looked out myself across the melancholy downs.

The moor is a place of 'dark imaginings', the Mire an image of the dangers that threaten the central characters in the book. For they might become victims to the morass of inexplicable legends and stories linked with the Baskerville name, surrendering to superstition, the light of scientific reason extinguished in the dark mysterious fogs of the Moor. As Watson looks out over the downs

> rain squalls drifted across their russet face and the heavy slate-coloured clouds hung low over the landscape, trailing in grey wreaths down the sides of the fantastic hills. In the distant hollow on the left, half-hidden by the mist, the two thin towers of Baskerville Hall rose above the trees.

Here is a suggestion of ghostly presences ('grey wreaths'), of things hidden in the mist and in hollows. In such an atmosphere of imponderables the mind could lose its powers of assessment and control.

Against these forces that could overwhelm a man or woman Watson sets his own sturdy no-nonsense common sense, his belief in the assessment of facts, though he himself lacks the intellectual capacity of Holmes to apply scientific method to the events of the book. So in his diary he writes:

A spectral hound which leaves material footmarks and fills the air with its howling is surely not to be thought of. Stapleton may fall in with such a superstition, and Mortimer also; but if I have one quality upon earth it is common sense, and nothing will persuade me to believe in such a thing. To do so would be to descend to the level of these poor peasants who are not content with a mere fiend-dog, but must needs describe him with hell-fire shooting from his mouth and eyes. Holmes would not listen to such fancies, and I am his agent.

It becomes significant that Stapleton, Mortimer and Frankland are all interested in science of one kind or another. Now Conan Doyle may have supplied each of them with hobbies and interests as a simple means of characterisation, but the fact remains that as we read the book we get an increasing impression of various rational systems set against the forces of the Moor. Mortimer is interested in the study of human skulls, Stapleton in botany and the collecting of moths and butterflies. Frankland is absorbed by the British law. Frankland's interest in the law threatens to 'swallow up the remainder of his fortune', suggesting that his search for a rational means of ordering human affairs will lead to self-destruction. We note the metaphor 'swallow up' and may be reminded of the Great Mire. It is unlikely that Conan Doyle deliberately employed this metaphor to relate Frankland's suicidal interest in litigation with the symbolic Mire, but the appropriateness of the phrase may perhaps have its source in the author's unconscious imaginative processes. Such speculation is given added weight when we turn to Stapleton, whose passion for collecting specimens takes him out on the Moor, where eventually he will be destroyed. His pursuit of botanical knowledge has something nervous, overly scrupulous, curiously manic about it, suggesting that, like Frankland's legal mania, it will also prove a destroyer. Stapleton's consuming passion is associated with the Mire in a direct way:

> ... a small fly or moth had fluttered across our path, and in an instant Stapleton was rushing with extraordinary energy and speed in pursuit of it. To my dismay the creature flew straight for the Great Mire, but my acquaintance never paused for an instant, bounding from tuft to tuft behind it, his green net waving in the air. His grey clothes and jerky, zigzag, irregular progress made him not unlike some huge moth himself. I was standing watching his pursuit with a mixture of admiration for his extraordinary activity and fear lest he should lose his footing in the treacherous Mire ...

By contrast Dr Mortimer's scientific interests allow him to work without fear on the Moor. So Watson tells us mid-way in the book:

> The other day—Thursday, to be more exact—Dr Mortimer lunched with us. He has been excavating a barrow at Long Down, and has got a prehistoric skull which fills him with great joy. Never was there such a single-minded enthusiast as he!

Single-minded, enthusiastic pursuit of truth is, it seems, to be distinguished from neurotic, disturbed scientific passion. It is closer to Watson's passion for common sense and Holmes's persistent attention to fact and detail.

Conan Doyle did not, however, write *The Hound of the Baskervilles* to develop and explore the theme of a conflict between supernatural powers and controlled, sensible, scientific enquiry, between Holmes and the Great Mire. Indeed a reader may in fact feel a little irritated that he failed to exploit to the full the symbolic and imaginative possibilities of his material. But to feel that would be to commit the error (see the warning against this, p.42) of criticising the work for failing to be what the author had no intention it should be—a serious novel. Rather, the suggestion of a serious subject matter helps to hold the reader's attention. Not only a taste for exciting, swift-moving action, but a need for thematic implication, is satisfied.

The fact that *The Hound of the Baskervilles* is an entertainment, not a serious novel, reveals itself in the book's controlling tone. The disturbing implications of the book's events are not allowed to interfere with the narrator's basic tone of voice. At times Watson gets depressed, frightened, angry, perplexed, but he is never allowed, often in the face of the most horrifying events, to lose his hold on an essential common sense which reveals itself in a steady, careful, occasionally dull-witted reportage. Watson is not altered by the events he witnesses, the implications of the action seem outside his intellectual and emotional capacities, and while we as readers may be aware of them, we are enabled to rest undisturbed, assured as we are of the certainties and decencies of life by the conventional, rather complacent tones of the book's narrator.

We don't know whether Conan Doyle was aware of the potential of his subject matter. The sense of implications that we have been considering may be simply (as was suggested above) an effect of the plot structure (the supernatural possibilities providing a way of spinning out the action) and a result of Conan Doyle's unconscious imaginative processes. What we do know is that the action is framed by Dr Watson's comfortable tones. So the dreadful events in Devonshire, our exposure to murderous evil in the person of Stapleton and to irrational forces symbolised by the Moor and the Great Mire, do not incline us to doubt, even at the end of Chapter 14, the certainties of everyday middle-class, urban life. Crime, evil, the irrational are seen as interruptions of the normal human order of things; we can enjoy the excitement of the story without being forced to ask whether the Mire represents a much more significant element in human experience than we normally like to admit. Instead, we are left with Holmes and Watson warming themselves at their fire in Baker Street, the Baskerville affair a matter for some regrets but also for curious speculation and satisfaction, before a relaxing evening at the theatre:

> It was the end of November, and Holmes and I sat, upon a raw and foggy night, on either side of a blazing fire in our room in Baker Street. Since the tragic upshot of our visit to Devonshire he had been engaged in two affairs of the utmost importance ... My friend was in excellent spirits over the success which had attended a succession of difficult and important cases, so that I was able to induce him to discuss the details of the Baskerville mystery.

SUMMARY: there are suggestions of serious themes in the book. These themes are: (*i*) The city and the country and (*ii*) Science and the supernatural. The controlling tone of the book does not allow these themes to disturb a reader unduly.

Literary techniques and strategies

The success of *The Hound of the Baskervilles* was based, as we have seen, on the qualities of the hero (see Part 1), on the author's skilful handling of the plot (see the commentaries in Part 2), on his capacity to make detective fiction entertaining and on his ability to suggest serious issues while actually ignoring them (see Part 3 above). Two technical aspects of the work may also account for its success: (*i*) The characterisation and (*ii*) The dialogue.

The characters in the book, as in all the Sherlock Holmes pieces, are really caricatures. Swiftly sketched when introduced, they do not develop or change. They serve as pegs upon which the exciting action is hung; they are cleverly painted cardboard figures moved about by the author as the plot demands. Conan Doyle does not employ many of the techniques developed by nineteenth-century novelists for the portrayal of human personality and psychology. There are no protracted passages where an apparently all-knowing author tells us how a character is feeling or changing. There are no interior monologues (passages where the author allows us to hear a character thinking). Nor indeed is dialogue much used to reveal personal likes and dislikes, opinions and ideas. At no point does the reader get a sense of the action slowing down to allow for a character's self-revealing utterance. Sharply drawn caricatures move swiftly through a series of blood-chilling events, keeping the narrative pace high.

The characters

Sherlock Holmes

We see Holmes in a number of different situations, at home, on the London streets, in Devonshire, none of which provides us with much information about his mental or emotional life. At all times, except at the climax, when he becomes rather anxious, he is the masterful sleuth applying his famous method. He is cleverly deductive and perceptive in the familiar way, he is decisive and forceful as in the following passage:

'Ha! Where is Barrymore?'
'He is in charge of the Hall.'
'We had best ascertain if he is really there, or if by any possibility he might be in London.'
'How can you do that?'
'Give me a telegraph form. "Is all ready for Sir Henry?" That will do. Address to Mr Barrymore, Baskerville Hall. Which is the nearest telegraph office? Grimpen. Very good, we will send a second wire to the postmaster, Grimpen: "Telegram to Mr Barrymore, to be delivered into his own hand. If absent, please return wire to Sir Henry Baskerville, Northumberland Hotel." That should let us know before evening whether Barrymore is at his post in Devonshire or not.

Elsewhere Sherlock Holmes is searchingly intense as an interrogator (note how he questions Dr Mortimer at the opening of Chapter 3, The Problem); he is cool and dispassionate ('Sherlock Holmes had, in a very remarkable degree, the power of detaching his mind at will'), he is suavely artistic ('The thing takes shape, Watson. It becomes coherent. Might I ask you to hand me my violin, and we will postpone all further thought upon this business...'). He is eccentric ('Through the haze I had a vague vision of Holmes in his dressing-gown coiled up in an armchair with his black clay pipe between his lips. Several rolls of paper lay around him'); he is physically very fit, has a cat-like love of personal cleanliness; he is mysterious ('One of Sherlock Holmes's defects—if, indeed one may call it a defect—was that he was exceedingly loath to communicate his full plans to any other person until the instant of their fulfilment'); condescending and rather self-righteous (to Mrs Laura Lyons 'I think that on the whole you have had a fortunate escape'); above all fearless and effective ('the next instant Holmes had emptied five barrels of his revolver into the creature's flank').

Dr Watson

Since Watson is the narrator we know more about his feelings than about the feelings of any other character in the book. However, his feelings are so uncomplicated and predictable that they suggest caricaturist techniques rather than a novelist's efforts to portray personality. Watson is adulatory of Holmes throughout, respectful, almost foolishly grateful for Holmes's compliments;

> He had never said as much before, and I must admit that his words gave me keen pleasure, for I had often been piqued by his indifference to my admiration and to the attempts which I had made to give publicity to his methods. I was proud, too, to think that I had so far mastered his system as to apply it in a way which earned his approval.

Watson is faithful, dogged, dimwitted (this aspect of his character is necessary to the prolonging of the action as has been suggested on p.15), conventionally chivalrous in a bachelor's way about women and embarrassed by strong emotions (when he sees Stapleton abusing Sir Henry in Chapter 9 he tells us 'What all this meant I could not imagine, but I was deeply ashamed to have witnessed so intimate a scene without my friend's knowledge.') Watson tends to anxiety, to befuddled worry, but he doesn't lack courage. A final sense of him is as a physical presence in the book. This is odd, since he doesn't describe his own appearance. However, his ponderous careful diary entries and his journal suggest a large bluff man who, when the need arises, can manage a fair turn of speed. A steady, useful man in a crisis is Watson. Remember Watson is the one who creeps down to Merripit House in Chapter 14, to reconnoitre and that he is a good deal faster in defence of Sir Henry than Lestrade, the professional policeman:

> Never have I seen a man run as Holmes ran that night. I am reckoned fleet of foot, but he outpaced me as much as I outpaced the little professional.

Dr Mortimer

Dr Mortimer is presented as an eccentric, brilliant, sceptical, scholarly enthusiast, a collector of odd lore. He is given the physical attributes of such a person and the quirks of manner and habit.

> He was a very tall, thin man with a long nose like a beak, which shot out between two keen, grey eyes, set closely together and sparkling brightly from behind a pair of gold-rimmed glasses. He was clad in a professional but rather slovenly fashion, for his frock-coat was dingy and his trousers frayed. Though young, his long back was already bowed, and he walked with a forward thrust of his head and a general air of peering benevolence.
>
> The man drew out paper and tobacco and twisted the one up in the other with surprising dexterity. He had long, quivering fingers as agile and restless as the antennae of an insect.
>
> He scribbled the appointment on his shirt-cuff and hurried off in his strange, peering, absent-minded fashion.

Sir Henry Baskerville

Sir Henry is portrayed as a strong, brave man. Somewhat rough in manner because of his adventurous life, he is nonetheless essentially a gentleman because of the noble blood that runs in his veins:

> He was a small, alert, dark-eyed man about thirty years of age, very sturdily built, with thick black eyebrows and a strong, pugnacious face. He wore a ruddy-tinted tweed suit, and had the weather-beaten appearance of one who has spent most of his time in the open air, and yet there was something in his steady eye and the quiet assurance of his bearing which indicated the gentleman.

The pugnacious, strong appearance is a clue to his determined character. He is not easily frightened: ' "There is no devil in hell, Mr Holmes, and there is no man upon earth who can prevent me from going to the home of my own people, and you may take that to be my final answer." His dark brows knitted and his face flushed to a dusky red as he spoke.' Sir Henry is properly delighted by his ancestral home when he arrives in Devon; he comes into his inheritance with an ambitious sense of his responsibilities (he intends to improve the estate) and a fine enthusiasm. ' "Baskerville Hall" said he. Its master had risen, and was staring with flushed cheeks and shining eyes.' Sir Henry is chiefly memorable for his native courage. ' "Give me another brandy, and I shall be ready for anything." '

Commentary · 53

Stapleton

Stapleton is portrayed as an intense, prim, eccentric botanist whose essential villainy is evident in the 'dry glitter in his eyes, and a firm set of his thin lips, which go with a positive and possibly harsh nature.' We first see him as

> a small, slim, clean-shaven, prim-faced man, flaxen-haired and lean-jawed, between thirty and forty years of age, dressed in a grey suit and wearing a straw hat.

He is knowledgeable, precise, rather argumentative, a little secretive in his conversation. Watson tells us that he is 'cool and unemotional', though we have seen him excitedly pursuing a specimen and he reacts with a frightening display of passion when he learns of Sir Henry's romantic feelings for his 'sister' (who is, of course, his wife). In the latter part of the book we see very little of Stapleton. He appears briefly on the scene when Selden is killed and Holmes, who now knows he is the criminal, remarks on his extraordinary coolness of nerve. Our last sight of him is with Sir Henry at the dinner in Merripit House on the night of his final disappearance.

Mrs Stapleton

Mrs Stapleton is merely the wronged misguided woman of romantic fiction. She is beautiful and exotic. There is an air of foreign mystery about her:

> ... she was darker than any brunette whom I have seen in England—slim, elegant and tall. She has a proud, finely cut face, so regular that it might have seemed impassive were it not for the sensitive mouth and the beautiful dark, eager eyes. With her perfect figure and elegant dress she was, indeed, a strange apparition upon a lonely moorland path.

So she is a fit object for Sir Henry's romantic affections and an appropriate victim for Stapleton's cruelty. Indeed Stapleton's treatment of such a 'very fascinating and beautiful woman' is apt testimony to his foul depravity. 'One towel passed round the throat, and was secured at the back of the pillar. Another covered the lower part of the face and over it two dark eyes—eyes full of grief and shame and a dreadful questioning—stared back at us. In a minute we had torn off the gag, unswathed the bonds, and Mrs Stapleton sank upon the floor in front of us. As her beautiful head fell upon her chest I saw the clear red weal of a whip-lash across her neck.'

Mrs Laura Lyons

This character is portrayed as an attractive but untrustworthy female. The first impression we have of her is confirmed by her subsequent part in the action:

> The first impression left by Mrs Lyons was one of extreme beauty. Her eyes and hair were of the same rich hazel colour, and her cheeks, though considerably freckled, were flushed with the exquisite bloom of the brunette, the dainty pink which lurks at the heart of the sulphur rose. Admiration was, I repeat, the first impression. But the second was criticism. There was something subtly wrong with the face, some coarseness of expression, some hardness, perhaps, of eye, some looseness of lip which marred its perfect beauty.

Frankland

'He is an elderly man, red-faced, white-haired and choleric' portrayed as an eccentric, 'spiteful old busybody' with a passion for the Law.

Barrymore

Barrymore appears as a loyal family retainer: 'He stood in front of us now with the subdued manner of a well-trained servant. He was a remarkable-looking man, tall, handsome, with a square black beard and pale distinguished features.' But he behaves very mysteriously and at one point we suspect he may be the villain.

Mrs Barrymore

Watson tells us she is 'a large, impassive, heavy-featured woman with a stern, set expression of mouth.' We learn little more of her except that she is emotional (she weeps at night) and is loyal to her convict brother, Selden.

Dialogue

Conan Doyle's ability to pen skilful, swift caricatures was employed in the service of a vigorous narrative pace (we don't have to wait while the author expansively treats of psychology and personality.) He employs dialogue to similar effect. John Fowles points out in his *Afterword* to the Pan edition of the book 'Conan Doyle's stroke of genius was in solving a problem that all novelists are familiar with; the natural incompatibility of dialogue and narrative ... Conversation and narrative are generally antipathetic, since continuously moving narrative displeases the writer's sense of realism; but if he concentrates on realistic conversation, which like the Wisht Hounds loves running round in circles, his narrative goes out of the window.' Conan Doyle's solution was to include a great deal of dialogue in his book while making certain that the dialogue always helps the plot along, keeps the narrative moving. Conversation, then, is not used to reveal personality, but neither is it used to describe settings or locales. Dialogue in *The Hound of the Baskervilles* maintains a flow of narrative information while allowing for a great deal of conversation. The conversation suggests a realistic element in the relationship between the two caricature figures of Holmes and Watson. Watson offers provocative platitudes and tentative suggestions, often to be met by Holmes's paradoxes, by his condescension, by his patronising approval. The pair behave in just the conventional way people tend to when they know each other well. There is a sense of epigrammatic pace in many of their exchanges; the dull Watson is a foil for the exact, laconic superiority of Holmes. And the epigrammatic pace is matched by the narrative pace, their conversations briskly keeping the story on the move.

The visual quality of *The Hound of the Baskervilles*

The fact that Conan Doyle employs caricature figures, a fast narrative pace and dialogue that, while usually aiding plot development, has attractions of its own, accounts for the highly visual nature of the book. A reader sees sharply defined figures moving quickly through a sequence of bizarre adventures; he hears the figures in conversation, but their conversation rarely departs from a conventional interchange between caricature images. Throughout the book characters and incidents are described with a great deal of visual impact.

In their original form the Sherlock Holmes stories were brilliantly illustrated. From the start Sherlock Holmes was both a character in a fiction and a visual image. Conan Doyle's main illustrator was Sydney Paget. He illustrated many of the author's Sherlock Holmes stories in *The Strand Magazine* and was responsible for Holmes's physical appearance. Conan Doyle wrote of how the illustrator altered his own conception of the detective:

> I saw him as very tall—'over six feet, but so excessively lean that he

seemed considerably taller' said *A Study in Scarlet*. He had, as I imagined him, a thin razor-like face, with a great hawk's bill of a nose, and two small eyes set close together on either side of it. Such was my conception. It chanced, however, that poor Sydney Paget, who, before his premature death drew all the original pictures, had a younger brother whose name, I think was Walter, who served him as a model. The handsome Walter took the place of the more powerful but uglier Sherlock.

Many of the crucial incidents in the stories were represented in illustrations, and as he reads *The Hound of the Baskervilles* a reader senses that the author is writing with an illustrator in mind. He provides an artist with scene after scene which might be pictorially represented: Holmes and Watson in Regent Street in pursuit of the mysterious cab and the black-bearded man; Watson and Sir Henry *en route* by horse-drawn carriage for Baskerville Hall; Barrymore welcoming them; the gloomy dining room; Barrymore staring out into the blackness of the moor; the solitary figure against the moon. (All these were illustrated in the original serial publication of the work). The scene where Watson comes upon Barrymore reads almost like notes from which an artist might work:

> A long black shadow was trailing down the corridor. It was thrown by a man who walked softly down the passage with a candle in his hand. He was in shirt and trousers, with no covering to his feet. I could merely see the outline, but his height told me that it was Barrymore. He walked very slowly and circumspectly, and there was something indescribably guilty and furtive in his whole appearance.

The image of the man on the granite tor in Chapter 9 is a moment of almost purely visual terror, the kind which would delight an illustrator:

> The moon was low upon the right, and the jagged pinnacle of a granite tor stood up against the lower curve of its silver disk. There, outlined as black as an ebony statue on that shining background, I saw the figure of a man upon the tor.

This visual aspect of Conan Doyle's work may well be its most remarkable feature. In a period when photography was very popular the author seems to have sensed the potential of highly visual literary works. He was sensitive, in modern terms, to the high informational content of visual images. For the visual image has an immediacy of impact, a quality of instantaneous significance that the written word cannot match. Conan Doyle wrote in a way that exploits this. His true originality was that at the very beginning of the age of mass society with its constant invention of advertising and propagandist images, its posters and signs that provide instant visual statements of ideas and concepts, he sensed the potentialities of the new age. So, while his work appealed to his contemporaries in their fears and aspirations, it was also in tune with things that were yet to be.

SUMMARY: (*i*) the figures in the book are caricatures; (*ii*) the dialogue is conventional though the relationship between Holmes and Watson has its realistic aspects. The dialogue is usually employed to maintain the narrative pace; (*iii*) the work is highly visual and (*iv*) Conan Doyle anticipated the age of the visual presentation of ideas and concepts.

Weaknesses of style, technique and plot

Many of the descriptive passages in the book are over-written. Conan Doyle obviously felt that he could not set his tale in Devonshire without describing the landscape and the ancestral home with which much of the action is associated. But the writing at such points is stodgy and dull. The author in straining to be effective has over-written, crowding his language with adjectives. Consider the following passage:

> The avenue opened into a broad expanse of turf, and the house lay before us. In the fading light I could see that the centre was a heavy block of building from which a porch projected. The whole front was draped in ivy, with a patch clipped bare here and there where a window or a coat-of-arms broke through a dark veil. From this central block rose the twin towers, ancient, crenellated and pierced with many loopholes. To right and left of the turrets were more modern wings of black granite. A dull light shone through heavy mullioned windows, and from the high chimneys which rose from the steep, high-angled roof there sprang a single black column of smoke.

Notice here the many descriptive words. These suggest the author painstakingly making notes as he examines the building; an impression of strain results. Notice also words like 'fading', 'draped', 'dark', 'dull', 'black'. These are supposed to create atmosphere, but how much more excitingly atmospheric are those passages in which the dialogue briskly terrifies us.

At moments the caricatures are merely mechanical puppets that the author uses when he needs a new character. So when Watson accompanies Stapleton to Merripit House the writing is mechanical; a dreary landscape is provided with its appropriate figure: 'An orchard surrounded it [the house] but the trees, as is usual upon the moor, were stunted and nipped, and the effect of the whole place was mean and melancholy. We were admitted by a strange, wizened, rusty-coated old manservant, who seemed in keeping with the house.' The manservant is not really required by the plot (though he crops up again as Stapleton's accomplice in Chapter 15). His main purpose here is to be 'in keeping with the house' which he is in far too mechanical and obvious a way.

The explanatory last chapter is rather a disappointment. We wonder how Stapleton imagined he could profit by his crime, for if it transpired after Sir Henry's death that his heir had been living nearby for two years under an assumed name, suspicion would inevitably fall upon him. Holmes's effort to avoid this problem is most unconvincing and one senses that Conan Doyle knows it is, for he hurries away from the point rather too glibly. As John Fowles has wittily put it 'I think I know why Conan Doyle sent Stapleton to a silent death in the Grimpen Mire; he was not a man who could have explained himself convincingly.'

However, despite these weaknesses *The Hound of the Baskervilles* is an extraordinarily entertaining piece of work. It is only in retrospect that problems about the plot (such as why it took Holmes so long to deal with a really rather simple case which he must have solved early on) begin to trouble the reader. Most of the caricatures are satisfyingly well-drawn and the absorbing pace of the narrative allows us to forgive the author his occasional passages of wordy, dull, descriptive prose. As an entertainment the book is to be judged a success; most people find it a great deal of fun.

Part 4

Hints for study

Take the four points outlined in Part 2 which suggested reasons for Holmes's popularity as a hero and apply them in detail to *The Hound of the Baskervilles*. The following are some suggestions as to how this might be done.

(1) Holmes's clear sense of right and wrong
This reveals itself in his treatment of Stapleton. He has no qualms about the villain's death, clearly believing that he was aptly punished for his misdeeds.
Make a list of all the incidents in the book which suggest Holmes's moral self-assurance.

(2) Holmes is an amateur and a gentleman
There are quite a number of occasions where Conan Doyle suggests this. Make a list of them. For example, you might examine Holmes's attitude to the professional policeman, Lestrade. Note also that there is no mention of a fee for his work on the case. He chooses to interest himself in the mystery of Sir Charles's death only because it fascinates him.

(3) Holmes is an individualist
Obviously the plot highlights this in placing Holmes alone on the moor for much of the book—he does not tell even Watson of his plans. Make a list of all the details in the book which suggest Holmes is a daring individualist who delights in working on his own.

(4) Holmes is a man of superior intellect and general cultivation
Make a list of the details which support this statement

When you have made these lists you will be well on the way towards a comprehensive understanding of the way Holmes is treated as the hero of the book. You will have basic material for answering questions like the following:

(1) In what ways is Sherlock Holmes made to seem remarkable in *The Hound of the Baskervilles*?
(2) Is Sherlock Holmes really the hero of *The Hound of the Baskervilles*?
(3) Can you account for the popularity of Sherlock Holmes with late Victorian readers?

The commentaries in Part 2 had much to say on the way Conan Doyle used the narrator, Dr Watson, to maintain tension and suspense by deliberately leading us away from the truth. Make your own list of all the occasions when the dim-witted Watson is used to conceal the truth or to confuse us about the cause of Sir Charles's death. In this way you will gather material for answering questions on the way Watson is used in the construction of the plot of the book. You must then make notes on Watson's personality considering:

(1) His attitude to Holmes and his relationship with the detective.
(2) His attitude to Sir Henry.
(3) His attitude to women.
(4) His attitude to the setting of the tale and to the dangers he faces here.
(5) His response to the revelation of Stapleton's villainy.
(6) The style of his diary and journal entries.

You will then have material for writing on Watson as the narrator of the book. You will understand his function in relation to the plot and will have a strong sense of the personality which Conan Doyle has given him. In recognising Watson's caricatured personality as the means whereby Conan Doyle tells us his tale you will understand why, although the book has its suggestion of thematic seriousness, it remains an entertainment. You will therefore be able to answer a question such as 'What is Dr Watson's function as narrator in *The Hound of the Baskervilles*?' by expanding on the following points

(1) **To maintain suspense.** He does this by: (*a*) Missing the obvious clues when they present themselves, (*b*) Following false leads in Holmes's absence, as with the Barrymore mystery; (*c*) Taking the supernatural possibilities seriously and responding to the eerie Devonshire setting.

(2) **To act as a foil for Sherlock Holmes's brilliance,** that is, allowing Holmes to seem a superior intellect in comparison with Watson's dull-witted pondering. In this section of your essay you might write on the style of Watson's journal and diary entries, noting their earnest, dogged, persistent worthiness, their concern to be accurate and comprehensive. By contrast with Watson's slow accumulation of information Holmes's instant grasp of the significance of details seems all the more intuitively brilliant.

(3) **To create the controlling tone of the book,** a tone that does not allow it to become too serious, too likely to disturb a reader. Watson, a solid, sane man of common sense, is the norm by which the terrible events in Devonshire are measured and seen to be abnormal.

Part 2, while attending to the role of Watson as narrator, also paid close attention to the plot structure of the book in general. We saw there that the plot of *The Hound of the Baskervilles* involved Conan Doyle in a number of problems. From early on Holmes knows that a natural hound lies behind the mystery and that Sir Henry's boot has been stolen to give the hound his scent. So someone is planning to kill him. It would not take a man of Holmes's ingenuity very long to find out who such might be among the relatively few Devonshire suspects. So Holmes must be removed from the forefront of the action there while Watson occupies centre-stage for much of the book. To compensate for a reader's disappointment at Holmes's absence Conan Doyle supplies him with (*i*) The Barrymore sub-plot and (*ii*) The supernatural possibilities and the eeriness of the Devonshire setting. These also keep our minds off Stapleton, the real villain, as Barrymore is portrayed in terms that make him seem much more worthy of suspicion than the botanist. But Holmes is kept in our minds through Watson writing to him.

With these facts as material you will certainly be able to deal with questions on Conan Doyle's skill with a plot. You might also, in dealing with questions on Conan Doyle's skilful handling of plot, point out how well he manages transitions in the action. At points where a reader's interest could diminish he always manages to introduce some new excitement. Pay attention to these transitions in the narrative. For example, when we learn the reason for Barrymore's behaviour in Baskerville Hall we are immediately intrigued by a strange figure on the moor. When, in Chapter 12, we realise that Stapleton is the villain, Conan Doyle counteracts any disappointment we might feel at the unravelling of the affair by providing the horror of Selden's death with the initial suspicion that it is Sir Henry who has been murdered.

In answering questions which allow you to deal with Conan Doyle's narrative skill you can draw on this material, as well as on the material relating to Dr Watson as narrator outlined above (p.60) Examples of such questions might be:

(1) How does Conan Doyle raise and maintain a reader's excitement in *The Hound of the Baskervilles*?
(2) How does Conan Doyle solve the problems in the plot of *The Hound of the Baskervilles*?
(3) Why is Sherlock Holmes absent from the action of *The Hound of the Baskervilles* for so long? How does Conan Doyle attempt to compensate for his absence? Is he successful?

You might also examine the role of the supernatural in the book. It serves various functions:

(1) It entertains through creating exciting feelings of horror.
(2) It helps to prolong the plot and maintain tension and mystery as demonstrated in Part 2.
(3) It suggests thematic significances as discussed in Part 3.

You might prepare for questions on this topic by making notes of those moments and sections in the book where the supernatural functions in these various ways, examining how the precise effects are achieved. Questions on this topic might be of the following type:

(1) To what extent is the supernatural important in *The Hound of the Baskervilles*?
(2) How does Conan Doyle treat the supernatural in *The Hound of the Baskervilles*?
(3) Examine the ways in which Conan Doyle combined a tale of the supernatural with a detective story in *The Hound of the Baskervilles*.
(4) To what extent would a reader be justified in seeing the conflict between science and superstition as a major theme of *The Hound of the Baskervilles*?

Select a passage in the book where dialogue is employed at length. Study the selected passage with the following questions in mind:

(1) What have we learned about the principal characters?
(2) In what ways is the book's plot carried forward by the dialogue in this passage? Make a detailed list of all the plot information contained in the dialogue and you will see how skilfully Conan Doyle uses dialogue in the interests of his narrative.
(3) In what ways does the dialogue entertain the reader while developing the plot?

In answering these questions you will be preparing to deal with examination questions on Conan Doyle's skill with dialogue.

One of the attractions of the Sherlock Holmes stories for the modern reader is their period charm, their capacity to suggest the atmosphere of a vanished age. Strictly speaking, this is a fairly limited sort of literary pleasure, but it would be narrow-minded and futile for the literary critic to attempt to belittle it. There is a nostalgic element to be derived from the images of late Victorian life in *The Hound of the Baskervilles* which has appealed to many twentieth century readers in the same way as costume dramas on television have done. The millions who watched *The Forsyte Saga* on television stations throughout the world were indulging a similar taste to those who enjoy in the Sherlock Holmes stories glimpses of life as lived by their grandfathers or great grandfathers.

Make a list of the places in the book where we can take pleasure in the suggestions of period charm, of those moments where the atmosphere of the past age is engagingly present. The following is a selection of such passages:

> He quickened his pace until we had decreased the distance which divided us by about half. Then, still keeping a hundred yards behind, we followed into Oxford Street and so down Regent Street. Once our friends stopped and stared into a shop window, upon which Holmes did the same. An instant afterwards he gave a little cry of satisfaction, and, following the direction of his eager eyes, I saw that a hansom cab with a man inside which had halted on the other side of the street was now walking slowly onwards again.

> Until we got three-quarters down Regent Street. Then my gentleman threw up the trap, and he cried that I should drive right away to Waterloo Station as hard as I could go. I whipped up the mare, and we were there under the ten minutes. Then he paid up his two guineas, like a good one, and away he went into the station.

> I knew that seclusion and solitude were very necessary for my friend in those hours of intense mental concentration during which he weighed every particle of evidence, constructed alternative theories, balanced one against the other and made up his mind as to which points were essential and which immaterial. I therefore spent the day at my club, and did not return to Baker Street until evening. It was nearly nine o'clock when I found myself in the sitting-room once more.

> 'And now, my dear Watson, we have had some weeks of severe work, and for one evening, I think we may turn our thoughts into more pleasant channels. I have a box for *Les Huguenots*. Have you heard the De Reszkes? Might I trouble you then to be ready in half an hour, and we can stop at Marcini's for a little dinner on the way?'

In considering the period atmosphere of the book, pay attention to the way in which old styles of life and modern ones intermingle. We are offered in the book a world of hansom cabs and horse-drawn wagonettes, as well as express trains, telegrams and modern print techniques. The book precisely suggests a late-Victorian atmosphere where old and new ways intermingled. Holmes was living at the end of one kind of world, the old land-based hierarchical English society, and at the beginning of the new highly industrial, technological, democratic, admass age that we have inherited. An impression of the transitional quality of his period emerges from the stories and from this book. An ancestral curse in rural Devonshire disturbs, but does not overturn, a world of scientific theory, railways, telegrams and newspapers. The Great Mire is centuries old, but Lestrade can be summoned down to Devonshire on the London evening express.

Study projects

(1) Try to read some of the short stories in which Sherlock Holmes appeared. Attempt a Sherlock Holmes story of your own. Here are some titles that you might use as the basis of a tale: The case of the missing mummy; The case of the frightened jockey; The disappearing Rembrandt; Holmes in Istanbul; Dr Watson's triumph.
(2) Much of *The Hound of the Baskervilles* is in dialogue. Try dramatising some of the main scenes with a friend who also knows the book. Consider how you would produce the book as a radio play. What kind of actors would you use for various characters (remember on radio it is the voice that counts)? What kind of music would you use? Do you know any piece of music that would be appropriate?
(3) Consider how the book could be filmed. What would be the problems facing a director? How would you solve them?
(4) If you are good at sketching try to illustrate a few of the incidents in the book.
(5) Read Wilkie Collins, *The Moonstone* and Edgar Allan Poe, *The Murders in the Rue Morgue*.
(6) You may become interested in the detective story as a form. Here are the names of some classic twentieth-century detective writers whose work you should look out: G.K. Chesterton (for his Father Brown stories), Agatha Christie, Dorothy Sayers, Edgar Wallace, Ronald Knox, Margery Allingham, Ellery Queen, Georges Simenon, Ngaio Marsh, Nicholas Blake, Michael Innes, Eric Ambler.
(7) It would be worthwhile to compare the detective story as written by Conan Doyle (Conan Doyle was among the first practitioners) with the more modern form of the thriller. Compare Sherlock Holmes with Ian Fleming's character, James Bond. You might also read the more serious kind of modern thriller or detective story and compare them with the Holmes series. Writers to look for are Raymond Chandler and John Le Carré.

Part 5

Suggestions for further reading

The text

The best text, since it contains Paget's illustrations, is *The Annotated Sherlock Holmes*, edited with an Introduction, Notes and Bibliography by William S. Baring-Gould, John Murray, London, 1968. This is a two volume work (*The Hound of the Baskervilles* is in Volume II) which contains much valuable information. The best easily available text is the Pan Book edition, London and Sydney, 1975. This edition has an excellent foreword and afterword by the contemporary English novelist, John Fowles.

Some books on Sherlock Holmes and Conan Doyle

BROWN, IVOR: *Conan Doyle*, Hamish Hamilton, London, 1972. A brief but refreshingly well-written, urbane biographical sketch.

HARRISON, MICHAEL: *In the Footsteps of Sherlock Holmes*, David and Charles, Newton Abbot: 1958, 1971. Whilst treating Holmes as almost a real person, this book, in a rather rambling way (as the title suggests) has a good deal to tell us about Holmes's London, its atmosphere and problems.

PEARSON, HESKETH: *Conan Doyle, His Life and Art*, Methuen, London, 1943. A sound study of the life and art.

Histories of detective fiction

HAYCRAFT, HOWARD: *Murder for Pleasure, The Life and Times of the Detective Story* with an introduction by Nicholas Blake, Peter Davies, London, 1942.

THOMSON, H. DOUGLAS: *Masters of Mystery: A Study of the Detective Story*, William Collins & Son, London, 1931.

For an excellent study of the rules governing modern detective fiction see *Cassell's Encyclopaedia of Literature*, edited by S.H. Steinberg, Cassell, London, 1953, pp.147–9.

The author of these notes

TERENCE BROWN was educated at Trinity College, Dublin, where he is currently Director of Modern English and a Fellow of the College. His publications include co-editing, with Alec Reid, *Time Was Away: The World of Louis MacNeice*, *Louis MacNeice: Sceptical Vision* and *Northern Voices: Poets from Ulster*. He is Secretary of the International Association for the Study of Anglo-Irish Literature and a founding member of the Institute for Arab-Irish Studies. He is currently co-editing a book on the Irish Short Story and writing a book on culture and society in modern Ireland.

YORK NOTES

The first 100 titles

CHINUA ACHEBE	*Arrow of God* *Things Fall Apart*
JANE AUSTEN	*Northanger Abbey* *Pride and Prejudice* *Sense and Sensibility*
ROBERT BOLT	*A Man For All Seasons*
CHARLOTTE BRONTË	*Jane Eyre*
EMILY BRONTË	*Wuthering Heights*
ALBERT CAMUS	*L'Etranger (The Outsider)*
GEOFFREY CHAUCER	*Prologue to the Canterbury Tales* *The Franklin's Tale* *The Knight's Tale* *The Nun's Priest's Tale* *The Pardoner's Tale*
SIR ARTHUR CONAN DOYLE	*The Hound of the Baskervilles*
JOSEPH CONRAD	*Nostromo*
DANIEL DEFOE	*Robinson Crusoe*
CHARLES DICKENS	*David Copperfield* *Great Expectations*
GEORGE ELIOT	*Adam Bede* *Silas Marner* *The Mill on the Floss*
T.S. ELIOT	*The Waste Land*
WILLIAM FAULKNER	*As I Lay Dying*
F. SCOTT FITZGERALD	*The Great Gatsby*
E.M. FORSTER	*A Passage to India*
ATHOL FUGARD	*Selected Plays*
MRS GASKELL	*North and South*

68 · List of titles

WILLIAM GOLDING	*Lord of the Flies*
OLIVER GOLDSMITH	*The Vicar of Wakefield*
THOMAS HARDY	*Jude the Obscure*
	Tess of the D'Urbervilles
	The Mayor of Casterbridge
	The Return of the Native
	The Trumpet Major
L.P. HARTLEY	*The Go-Between*
ERNEST HEMINGWAY	*For Whom the Bell Tolls*
	The Old Man and the Sea
ANTHONY HOPE	*The Prisoner of Zenda*
RICHARD HUGHES	*A High Wind in Jamaica*
THOMAS HUGHES	*Tom Brown's Schooldays*
HENRIK IBSEN	*A Doll's House*
HENRY JAMES	*The Turn of the Screw*
BEN JONSON	*The Alchemist*
	Volpone
D.H. LAWRENCE	*Sons and Lovers*
	The Rainbow
HARPER LEE	*To Kill a Mocking-Bird*
SOMERSET MAUGHAM	*Selected Short Stories*
HERMAN MELVILLE	*Billy Budd*
	Moby Dick
ARTHUR MILLER	*Death of a Salesman*
	The Crucible
JOHN MILTON	*Paradise Lost I & II*
SEAN O'CASEY	*Juno and the Paycock*
GEORGE ORWELL	*Animal Farm*
	Nineteen Eighty Four
JOHN OSBORNE	*Look Back in Anger*
HAROLD PINTER	*The Birthday Party*
J.D. SALINGER	*The Catcher in the Rye*
SIR WALTER SCOTT	*Ivanhoe*
	Quentin Durward

List of titles

WILLIAM SHAKESPEARE	*A Midsummer Night's Dream*
	Antony and Cleopatra
	Coriolanus
	Cymbeline
	Hamlet
	Henry IV Part I
	Henry V
	Julius Caesar
	King Lear
	Macbeth
	Measure for Measure
	Othello
	Richard II
	Romeo and Juliet
	The Merchant of Venice
	The Tempest
	The Winter's Tale
	Troilus and Cressida
	Twelfth Night
GEORGE BERNARD SHAW	*Androcles and the Lion*
	Arms and the Man
	Caesar and Cleopatra
	Pygmalion
RICHARD BRINSLEY SHERIDAN	*The School for Scandal*
JOHN STEINBECK	*Of Mice and Men*
	The Grapes of Wrath
	The Pearl
ROBERT LOUIS STEVENSON	*Kidnapped*
	Treasure Island
JONATHAN SWIFT	*Gulliver's Travels*
W.M. THACKERAY	*Vanity Fair*
MARK TWAIN	*Huckleberry Finn*
	Tom Sawyer
VOLTAIRE	*Candide*
H.G. WELLS	*The History of Mr Polly*
	The Invisible Man
	The War of the Worlds
OSCAR WILDE	*The Importance of Being Earnest*

Notes